DO YOU
KNOW YOUR
PEOPLE ?

INDIA • SINGAPORE • MALAYSIA

I0479640

Notion Press

No.8, 3rd Cross Street
CIT Colony, Mylapore
Chennai, Tamil Nadu – 600004

First Published by Notion Press 2020
Copyright © Shashikant Dabral 2020
All Rights Reserved.

ISBN 978-1-64919-501-2

This book has been published with all efforts taken to make the material error-free after the consent of the author. However, the author and the publisher do not assume and hereby disclaim any liability to any party for any loss, damage, or disruption caused by errors or omissions, whether such errors or omissions result from negligence, accident, or any other cause.

While every effort has been made to avoid any mistake or omission, this publication is being sold on the condition and understanding that neither the author nor the publishers or printers would be liable in any manner to any person by reason of any mistake or omission in this publication or for any action taken or omitted to be taken or advice rendered or accepted on the basis of this work. For any defect in printing or binding the publishers will be liable only to replace the defective copy by another copy of this work then available.

DO YOU
KNOW YOUR
PEOPLE?

Master the Management of Team Members

A Manager's Handbook
For Effective People Management

SHASHIKANT DABRAL

INDIA • SINGAPORE • MALAYSIA

INDICACADEMY

INDIC PLEDGE

———◆◆———

- *I celebrate our civilisational identity, continuity & legacy in thought, word and deed.*

- *I believe our indigenous thought has solutions for the global challenges of health, happiness, peace, and sustainability.*

- *I shall seek to preserve, protect and promote this heritage in doing so,*
  - *discover, nurture and harness my potential,*
  - *connect, cooperate and collaborate with fellow seekers,*
  - *be inclusive and respectful of diverse opinions.*

ABOUT INDIC ACADEMY

———◆◆———

Indic Academy is a non-traditional 'university' for traditional knowledge. We seek to bring about a global renaissance based on Indic civilizational and indigenous thought. We are pursuing a multidimensional strategy across time, space and cause by establishing centers of excellence, transforming intellectuals and building an ecosystem.

Indic Academy is pleased to support this book.

To my Mom

Contents

Preface

People management is a never-ending learning process. This is the uniqueness of the subject. It is rare to find two people who think alike. This makes the job of understanding and managing people unique. If no two people think alike, then it is likely that they would also react differently to different situations. Consequently, as a manager or supervisor, it is very challenging for a person to communicate, manage and get people to align themselves to one goal.

Many books have been written on leadership, how to manage people and styles of leadership. These books are informative and put forward several concepts in front of us, relating to leadership and people management. One is often left with a feeling that most of these books are at a concept level (at a very high level) and they do not give us tips on small steps that we can implement on a day-to-day basis. Managing people to build an organization and achieving organization goals is a challenging task. One needs to bear in mind that different people react differently and to a large extent, culture and traditions have a major bearing on it.

This book is based purely on my personal experience of over 21 years in building teams and managing people. It does not in any manner challenge anything said or written by anybody in any other book. This book will give readers tips on how I dealt with people issues and present my understanding of managing people and situations involving people.

Since a manager's/supervisor's work involves managing people, they will have a group of people (immediate team members) in their team and as mentioned above, all team members will be unique in their thinking and understanding. This would mean that the manager would have to understand each person and their ticking points to manage them. It is a tough job and to add to this challenge, there will always be a few new team members joining the team, while some existing employees leave the team. This makes people management a never-ending learning process.

The expectations of employees from an organization and their feelings are the same irrespective of their level or designation. To a large extent, for team members, the Supervisors/Managers are the organization and their actions have a direct impact on the team members and their career plans.

For ease of understanding:

1. *I have addressed a person who has more than one person reporting to him as a Team Leader/Supervisor and this does not refer to a designation. This would cover all of us who have a team reporting to us at any level.*

2. *I have referred to all employees as "he" (except in specific case studies, where the names are changed). This does not indicate any gender discrimination or bias and is purely meant for ease of writing.*

Acknowledgements

Since this book is based on my personal experience, all the people who worked with me throughout my career have contributed to the book in a way, either directly or indirectly.

It would not be possible to list all of them and hence I would like to thank all my colleagues, team members and Managers who were a part of my career journey. It is the learning I gathered while working with them about managing people that I am sharing in the form of "Do you know your people?".

Approach of the Book

This book is written in a simple manner by highlighting an issue as the title of the chapter, presenting the topic from an organization's point of view, and subsequently providing inputs and tips for middle management personnel to follow on a day-to-day basis. This book will not provide any quick fix/magical formula to its readers but will probably equip them with one additional way of dealing with issues related to people in their team. The book is written in a comprehensible language, with no corporate or management jargon. Middle management personnel will find it easy to understand. Furthermore, to make the points easy to relate to, I have narrated a few of my personal experiences as examples, so that the readers can relate them to their work environment easily.

Why People Join Organizations?

Every individual has his own reasons for wanting to join an organization. This sounds simple but understanding this forms the basis of how one manages people. Different people have different needs, aspirations and as a supervisor, one needs to be attentive and sensitive about it. If a person has an option of joining any company, then why would he choose your company?

A few reasons include:

- Brand name
- Good salary
- Plain need of job
- Only job that person could get
- Good reputation, though not the biggest brand or Biggest Brand
- Attractive office
- Five-day week with fixed weekend off's

- Friend /relatives working in the organization

- Role

I am sure we can add a few more points to this list.

All the reasons mentioned above are good to create excitement and curiosity in a person to apply for a job in an organization. Once the prospective employee applies, his process of evaluating the company starts in terms of:

- How his application is handled?

- How the ambiance of the office is?

- How positive the interview process is?

- How much time the organization takes to communicate the outcome?

For any employee/applicant to make up his mind to join an organization, the following points are important:

- Application handling

- The interview process (*Which can go into several rounds depending on the skill sets required*)

- Joining/induction process

- Culture of the organization

- Accessibility of information

- Performance management system

- Growth policy of the organization

Application Handling

For a prospective employee, the recruitment team of an organization is the face of the organization. How they deal with the applicants can make them either accept the offer or turn it down.

In the last few years, recruitment has become a challenging and stressful job. This is one department in most organizations, that is constantly under pressure. The recruitment policy manuals should have details of the entire recruitment process flow. A few good practices are:

1. Every application received by the organization from all sources, needs to be acknowledged, irrespective of the status of the application. The status refers to whether the organization is considering or rejecting the application.

   Intimate the time frame to the applicant in terms of how soon he can expect to hear from the organization, probable date of interview, how many rounds of interviews he will need to go through and details about the role.

   Information on the office location with landmark, Geo code of the address, whom to meet at reception, dress code and list of documents that the candidate needs to carry for the interview, should also be provided.

2. While making an offer, enough notice period should be given to the applicants to join the organization. It is necessary for an organization to insist on the prospective employee completing all relieving formalities in his previous organization.

   When an organization insists on this, it is creating an expectation in the prospective employee that the same will be expected from them while leaving this organization too.

Interview Process

It is very important for an organization to demonstrate punctuality, if the same is expected from the employees. If a candidate is given a time, then it needs to be adhered to. If due to any unavoidable reasons, it is not possible, then the applicant needs to be informed of the same.

While an applicant is waiting for his interview, he is observing the facility, how everybody around him is being treated and how the employees of the organization are moving about in the premises. All these things have an impact on the prospective employee to form an impression about the organization.

A few things an organization can do in this direction:

- While sending the interview invite, send the map location of the office through email and WhatsApp so that it is easy for the candidate to locate the office/ interview venue.

- Name and contact details of the person the candidate should contact at the reception/security.

- Seating/waiting area needs to be comfortable and bright, in terms of lighting and colour.

- Keep newspapers and some magazines in the waiting area. *(General information or brochures of the organization or company magazines are ideal).*

- If there is visual media in the waiting area, the management's address to teams, interview of team members and employee event videos can be played.

- Provide the seating area with drinking water facility. Tea/coffee would be an additional comfort.

- Provide the waiting area with neatly maintained washrooms.

- All personnel interacting with the applicants need to be polite.

- All HR/Admin personnel interacting with the applicants need to introduce themselves. The applicants should know whom they are talking to in the organization.

- At no point, the applicant should be made to feel inferior due to his personality or due to the outcome of the interview. Regardless of whether the applicant is selected or rejected they need to be given respect as a person.

- Maintain a positive environment all through the waiting and interview process.

- Make all the applicants feel that the organization values their time and thank them for their interest.

- If the candidate is to appear for more than one round of interview, the same must be informed while calling the applicant for the interview. This will help them plan their day accordingly.

- After every round of interview, they need to be informed of the result and details of the subsequent interview round (*Information about the date and time of the next round if it is not on the same day and details of the person who would be taking the interview, if possible*).

- Be very clear while communicating the outcome of the interview to the applicant. It is always good to communicate clearly and politely so that the applicant does not build any false hopes. At the same time, the applicant should not be hurt, if he is not selected.

- If an offer is being made, a note should be made of all points agreed upon. Summarize it to the prospective employee. The key points that must be included are:

  - Level at which the employee will join.

  - Fixed and variable salary component.

  - Performance appraisal cycle and probation period.

- Function in which the employee would work, shift/ work timings, weekly off(s) and leave policy.

- Notice period, if the employee decides to quit or the employee is asked to leave by the organization.

- The joining date, time, who to meet for the joining formalities and lastly, a list of all the documents the applicant needs to bring while joining.

Most organizations do not give importance to communicating to the applicant, the outcome of the interview, especially if the applicant is being rejected. One letter conveying politely that in the current situation the organization is not able to accommodate the candidate, or the organization is not able to match the candidate's qualification and work experience to any open position, would help in building a positive image of the organization.

After the interview process, if selected, the applicant reports in on the joining date. The fact that the applicant has reported to join would mean that he would have done his homework regarding details about the organization, the function in which he would be working, his immediate supervisor and about the team and its work culture. While the employee is settling in the organization, he is looking for reasons to validate his decision to join or stay in the organization. The first month of the prospective employee is very important and can lead to early attrition.

Joining Process/Induction Process

The applicant now becomes an employee and comes with enthusiasm and expectations on the first day to the organization. Make him feel welcomed in the group. The transition from a prospective employee to a productive employee must be smooth and monitored periodically. Few standard practices are:

- Common induction of all new employees/joinees from all departments on the day of joining. Introduce them to each other.

- An HR personnel dedicated to take care of all the joining formalities.

- Welcome speech/introduction by the CEO or top management personnel. This serves as an indication to employees that the top management is involved with them.

- Formal induction by HR.

- Presentations by all the Function Heads/Managers.

- Tour of the office premises.

- Informal introduction to their supervisor.

- Setting up the employee ID and basic requirements in the first two days, while the employees are being inducted by HR (If the induction process is going to take more than a day) or else all the basic set up has to be done by the time employee reports in for joining.

- A session to end the induction to answer their queries and doubts.

- Give them contact details of all the people they need to get in touch with for assistance related to administration, HR, Finance, and their work.

- Few organizations have the culture of immediate managers connecting with the team member soon after the prospective employee commits to a joining date and keeping in touch with them till they get on board.

While recruiting Senior Management personnel a few organizations have a practice of sending a bouquet and welcome card to the prospective employee, signed by the head of their department.

It is important for the existing employees/team members to be sensitive to the needs of the new team members and the hand holding process should be smooth so that the new employee adjusts to the organization easily.

Culture of the Organization

This topic will be covered in detail in the subsequent chapter. At this stage, it means how the employee is introduced to the culture of the organization. This is about laying down the organization's basic expectations from employees and setting their expectations right.

The new employee should be informed about the organization's purpose, vision, mission, code of conduct and the core values.

Detailing of the daily activities, escalation procedures, reporting structure etc, is best done in the form of a session conducted by the function head along with the HR personnel and this should be preferably done in an interactive manner.

Few policies like the code of conduct, dress code and leave policy should be read out and clarified rather than just handing over the document or giving the URL link to access the policy.

Accessibility of Information

It would be good, if a new employee gets to know in the initial period, what information is accessible to him and how he can access the same. The new employee needs to be given details of the policies applicable to him during his tenure in the organization. This is done by a few organizations in the form of giving a starter kit to the new employees. *(This kit usually contains an employee handbook with details of all policies and code of conduct along with a notepad and pen for making notes during the induction period. In addition, some organizations provide the new employees with a bag or a t-shirt with the firm's logo.)* A few organizations provide all this information on the organization intranet.

Performance Management System

Employees need to know what is expected of them, in clear measurable terms and in the form of a document. How it would result in rewards/returns for them? The performance management system needs to be explained clearly to all new employees. The targets/expectations are to be laid down in a measurable manner.

There must be a document on the performance appraisal system providing details pertaining to the periodicity of the cycle (bi-annual or annual), rating scale, appraisal methodology and the time frames. The Key Deliverables or Key Result Areas applicable to their role should be handed over to them during the training period. These can be provided online and need not necessarily be in the form of a physical document.

Growth Policy of the Organization

Employees need to know the promotion policy of the organization. The promotion policy should state details pertaining to:

- The qualification required to move to a level
- Number of years of experience required

- Skill sets and experience required in the specific area

- Performance rating required to move to the next level or between levels

- The minimum tenure of the employee in the organization or in the specific role

If the organization has an internal job posting, then the details of the process of job postings need to be explained.

At this stage, the real dynamics of an organization and people management come into play. The new employee starts observing the work culture, individual growth plans, his supervisor, how his work relates to the organization goals and to his team.

I take pride in mentioning that during my work tenure I had the opportunity of working with a couple of big organizations and most of the above-mentioned points were put in practice in these organizations. As a result of this, whenever I interacted with the new joinees in my organization, I would hear positive feedback about our practices and comments about the absence of these practices in their previous organizations.

It is common for employees to remember and talk about how they were initially introduced into the organization, how they had met their team and immediate supervisor for the first time.

The journey starts at this stage, when the employee goes through the joining formalities in the organization. If at this stage, he feels welcome and good to be on board, he starts on a positive note. He starts understanding the organization culture and how his role would place him in the team. From this stage, these points are constantly playing in the employee's mind.

Let us understand how a Team Leader/Supervisor can make the initial experience a good one for all the newly inducted employees.

For Team Leaders/Supervisors

> **Make the new employee comfortable and welcomed in your team.**

Every time a person joins a new organization, he comes with much anxiety about the company and the team. Making the new team member feel comfortable and welcome, gets rid of all the anxieties and the team member looks forward to starting his career in the organization. In the absence of this comfort, the new employee starts harbouring all kinds of fears, insecurities and starts wondering if the organization is the right place for him to work.

> **The team leader should get to know the employee, introduce himself as a person first and later as a professional.**

The team leader should not restrict the introduction to only professional details but should also share a little information about his personal self, in terms of his qualifications, college, previous work details and a little about his family.

This may not be significant in the western culture but in the Indian context, if one does not talk a bit about his personal details, like his family, hobbies, interests and other things which one generally likes to talk about, the employee feels that the organization has a very formal culture. In a purely formal environment, an employee feels that he is considered a tool and not a human being. In our culture, we like to talk, socialize at a personal level and when this does not happen it makes us uncomfortable. As a Team Leader, one needs to be aware of this and be sensitive about it.

➢ **Introduce the new employee to the team not just by mentioning his name and role but also add a little information about his previous work (academic achievements in case of a fresher), personal achievements and his hobbies.**

An employee likes to be treated as a human being, not just as a tool to achieve the organization goals and when we talk about his hobbies, previous work experience and achievements, then we are accepting him as a person, introducing him as a person and not just as a tool. At this point, it would be good to have the fresher join the team WhatsApp group, if any, so that he feels included in the team.

➢ **Check on the induction batches during training.**

The new employee should not get a feeling that the people in the organization are polite and caring only till they get them to join the organization. Offering help and assistance during the initial period demonstrates that the organization is concerned about them, their comfort in the initial phase, learning process and performance. This is particularly necessary in case of outstation employees; they would require assistance in finding suitable accommodation. They should not be left alone to do it all by themselves.

> ➤ **Once the training is completed, during On the Job Training (OJT), assign a senior who is not only good at work but is also assertive, as a buddy/coach to the new employees.**

Handholding sets the context for the new employee; he starts imbibing the organization culture and values from the assigned buddy. A positive person will influence the new employee positively, while a negative buddy will feed only negativity to a new employee.

> ➤ **The first three months are critical in shaping the employee's view of the organization culture. Utilize this time effectively.**

On a weekly basis, for the first three months, the Team Leader and the HR team should meet the new employees once, to collect feedback and offer support and assistance. This is both in the interest of the organization and the new employee. The organization can monitor the training and learning curve so that the new employee gets the required support to get up to speed and become productive. This approach will also provide inputs on the changes/improvements that can be done in the OJT process.

> ➤ **Formal feedback on the new employee's performance during the training and OJT will give them a feeling that their progress is being monitored and the organization really wants to help them get up to speed.**

This makes the employee realize that his performance and development is not his individual responsibility, as the organization is keen to make the employee learn, develop, and succeed. These feedback meetings will also help in getting to know the areas where the new team member needs support and ensuring that he gets the support in time to finish his learning.

> ➤ **The team leader should lay down the rules by which he operates, during the initial days of the new employee.**

If the employee gets to know the Do's and Don'ts of a team and is introduced to the best practices established by them, it will help him learn without making mistakes and scale up faster. This sets the expectations clearly in the new employee's mind and it helps him adjust to the organization/team accordingly.

> ➤ **Few Team Leaders take the new team members out for lunch/dinner after successful completion of the**

training. It gives them an opportunity to get to know their team members better.

This helps the team leader establish a good equation and understanding with the new team members, when they work together. Employees are likely to be more comfortable and they open-up during an informal conversation, especially if it is in an outside setting.

➢ **Few things a team leader can do to make team members comfortable:**

1. Provide your contact number and email ID to all the new employees so that they can mail you or call you in case of any difficulty.

2. Encourage them to differ from others, if they feel that something is not right as per their understanding or if they have a better idea. Of course, also tell them how to go about doing it and to not just challenge anybody and everybody in any forum.

3. Encourage them to clear their doubts without fear of being ridiculed. Let them know it is okay to commit mistakes while attempting out-of-the-box solutions.

4. Communicate that you would like to get suggestions on how improvements can be made to the work process and culture.

5. Explain the escalation matrix. If possible, introduce them to all the relevant people.

6. Have an Open House session with them and address all their doubts and concerns.

7. Lastly, it is always helpful for a team leader/ supervisor to be cheerful and have a good sense of humour, someone who makes work enjoyable rather than stressful and boring.

The above-mentioned seven suggestions will help provide necessary information to the new employees and make them feel that they can contribute to the progress of the organization in their own small way. It will make them feel that they are a valued member of the corporate family.

At this stage, the employees have joined the organization and are more or less sure that this is where they want to work. Now, let us try to understand what will keep them in the organization, what needs to be done by the organization and supervisor to retain and get the best out of them.

Space to Make Notes for Readers

_____

_____

_____

_____

_____

_____

_____

_____

_____

_____

_____

_____

_____

_____

What Retains Them?

At a broad level, there are three things that help retain an employee with an organization for a longer period.

1. Business plans & individual growth

2. Work culture/atmosphere

3. Value addition

Business Plans & Individual Growth

We all want to grow, grow in our own work area, grow in terms of designation, responsibilities, and money. If an employee can see growth of the organization, he would like to be a part of the entity, if he has the required potential and capability, he will get his share of growth too. Please note that this will not happen only with existing employees but also with new employees who have their own growth plans and are ambitious.

The problem starts when an employee is not aware of the organization's business plan and potential for growth.

The employee starts feeling restless and starts looking out for growth outside the organization/industry. It is very important for the organization, to communicate on a periodic basis, about the industry scenario, impact of the same on the organization, the organization's performance in the last quarter, annually and the business plans/targets for the next quarter/year. This needs to be further elaborated in terms of how it would benefit the employees in the form of salary revision, bonus declaration or the organization's expansion plans and growth opportunities. This serves as a reassurance to the employee that his growth plans can be met in the organization.

Many organizations have periodic, company-wide staff meetings to communicate this to the employees. Some organizations call these meetings **'All Hands Meeting,'** some as **'Town Hall'** and some call it **'Annual Staff Meeting.'** Some organizations conduct these meetings on a quarterly basis, while others prefer to do it on a half yearly or annual basis.

The broad agenda of all the above-mentioned meetings is:

- Plan Vs Actuals of the last months/quarter or year

- Achievements of the last months/quarter or year

- Performance of all the functions/departments during the period

- How the organization's performance is beneficial to all (in terms of the bonus or hikes that are likely to be declared/approved)

- Plans for the next three to six months or year

- Targets for all the functions/departments

- Top performing employees for that period (A *few organizations do this to provide the top performers the recognition in front of the whole company. A few organizations have a separate awards night for this purpose)*

- Expansion plans

This information provides the employee an update on the organization's performance, helps him plan for his own milestones for the year and map out career advancement in the organization based on the plans presented.

Work Culture/Atmosphere

If an employee does not like to work in the organization, no amount of motivation techniques or money can keep him in the organization. The worst scenario is when he stays for the sake of money without performing up to his potential. The first and foremost thing an organization needs to achieve is to make its employees feel like coming to work daily.

Thanks to the BPO industry, we find most organizations trying to have an open and informal culture at work. This in no way means that the organization follows an approach of **'all fun and no work'.** Rather, it indicates that it is very important for organizations to have the **FUN** element added to the work culture. Employees will look forward to coming to work daily and not come just for the sake of marking their attendance, which translates to a day's pay.

Respect for All

This sounds basic but if one needs to know the true culture of an organization, then he must observe how the senior most *(starting right from the CEO to all the management team members)* people of the organization behave with the most junior staff/contract workers of the company. *(This could include the house keeping staff, company car drivers or security staff).* An organization must respect people right from the lowest level to the topmost and this can happen only top-down. Every employee, irrespective of his level, age, sex, religion, or his performance, deserves to be respected as a person.

Build an Atmosphere of Trust

It is very important for an employee to trust the organization. They must believe that all the communication and policies laid down are implemented in real terms and practised. They are not just a piece of documentary *artwork.* An employee needs to have trust and faith in the organization's capability and track record of achieving the goals and targets laid down, so that he is excited to be a part of the organization and its growth. This trust can be built only by sharing with employees the plans and milestones achieved on a regular basis. If the trust element is missing, then even if the organization has been able to achieve the goals and targets set for the last quarter/year and has set aggressive targets for the next quarter/year, it doesn't excite the employee, as he feels that he won't get his share in the organization's achievements.

Fun at Work

Work culture and atmosphere does not only retain employees, but it also provides them with fuel to outperform themselves. When an employee comes to work, he should come with zeal and enthusiasm to do his best.

A few good practices in this direction include holding competitions internally, between and within teams, on things other than work: *(Though all the below suggestions sound like silly activities, they do have an impact on the young employees):*

- Decorations for festivals
- Painting competitions

- Drawing

- Singing and dance competitions

There can be enough creativity in coming up with the prize too, so that this motivates all employees to participate voluntarily rather than through coercion. The wining team could be given movie tickets, lunch with the business head or CEO or a gift voucher which they could utilize for their family. These activities create a festive atmosphere in the workplace and the employee enjoys celebrating the festival with his office family members.

If I enjoy my work then I will give it my best, and this is very important for any team.

Extra-curricular Activities

Some organizations encourage the formation of sports teams based on the region's favourite sport and conduct regular sports events to recharge their employees. Regular picnic tours/outings for teams are organized and encouraged by the management. All the above-mentioned activities bring employees together, creating a bond and boosting team spirit. It re-energizes the employees and makes them feel that there is more than work in the organization for them to look forward to. These activities can be either outdoor activities or indoor board games or it can be a combination of both. The idea is to create enough buzz, increase the energy level of the teams and get the competitive juices flowing.

Value Addition

It is common for people to leave a well settled and good paying job, the reason being almost always the same: "I do not find any value addition to myself".

All of us want to learn more, earn more and do more than what we were doing earlier. If an employee feels that his role is heading to a dead end, he is likely to leave.

An organization must ensure that their people are constantly getting enriched. Doing small things like the following, can help in that direction:

- Send employees for training programs relevant to their work area.

- Conduct soft skills training.

- Motivational talks by renowned people.

- Many organizations go the extra mile, providing tips to employees on how to get more out of life through yoga or art of living classes, on a regular basis.

- Job rotation can be effectively used to make employees multi-skilled.

- Run some higher education sponsorship programs by collaborating with good educational institutions.

- Help them acquire new skill sets through deputation programs or by providing them with in house training.

- Put in place a career plan / path for all employees.

Some people feel that the organization's brand name is one reason why an employee would like to work with the organization. This might be true in the short term, as an employee would like to increase his market value by getting the brand name on his resume. If this were true, then all big brands should ideally have 0% attrition. Alternatively, if an employee has joined the organization for the sake of including the brand name on his resume, but after joining he finds all the other factors mentioned above in the organization, then it is quite possible that he may stay and the chances of his exit reduce substantially.

During my work tenure, I had come across quite a few team members, who joined the organization for a short period as they had plans to pursue higher studies and the current job was meant to be just a stop gap arrangement. Once they joined the organization, they realized that the work atmosphere was good and they enjoyed coming to work on a daily basis. Consequently, they changed or rather they altered their plans to pursue higher studies and started pursuing the same along with the job through the medium of correspondence courses.

Let Us Go Through a Case

Sunita had moved to a new city and joined my organization as her husband had got a transfer from another city. During the 10 months Sunita had worked with the organization, her performance was good, and thus she was assigned additional responsibilities. *She often used to express her happiness by saying that she had never been happy working for any other organization in the past. One day, Sunita told me that her husband got a promotion and was transferred to another city. I told Sunita she was doing an excellent job and that the organization had good career plans for her. She took two days' time to discuss the situation with her husband and get back to me on what they planned to do about the move. Subsequently, she informed me that she decided to stay back in the city while her husband would go forward with his transfer. At a later stage, they would decide if she would continue or move.*

During this period, I had the opportunity to meet Sunita's husband when he had come for a family-day visit to our office. He said, "I can see that she is enjoying her work more than any of her previous jobs. I want her to stay back here till I check the new branch and settle down there". After about a month Sunita resigned and joined her husband but I was happy that my team leaders were surely doing something good due to which team members enjoyed their work and felt good about working in the organization.

Learnings from the Incident

- If team members enjoy working in the team/ organization, they will give their best.
- If the work culture is good, the team member will not leave the organization, unless he has some other pressing and genuine reason.

- If the team member feels that his efforts are suitably recognized and rewarded, then he will stay with the organization due to his trust in the organization and its policies.

- If a team member feels that he is learning new things in the organization and that is in turn making him a better person/professional, then he will want to stay with the organization. Remember, in the above incident, the team member was keen to stay back for two reasons:

  1. She liked the work culture and she enjoyed her work

  2. She was aware of the greater responsibilities given to her and the career plan put in place for her.

For Team Leaders/Supervisors

➢ **Ensure that all employees have their respective list of key deliverables with them and have understood them clearly.**

This is a basic expectation of any employee. He must know what is expected of him and how his performance will be measured. In the absence of this, the employee will either come to work just to pass his time or he will work as per his discretion. Subjectivity or ambiguity regarding a person's deliverables leads to chaos, gossip and wastage of the organization's money and resources.

➤ **As far as possible, maintain a lively work environment in your team all the time.**

A lively and positive environment at the workplace, induces positive energy and enthusiasm among employees. On the other hand, a tense or negative environment makes an employee dull and stressed. An employee spends a major portion of his waking hours in office and when he is stressed/unhappy in that environment, he does not give his best, which means he will not perform to his fullest potential and will constantly keep looking for excuses to abstain from work. On the other hand, if he is happy coming to work and looks forward to coming to work, he will give his best and will not miss a day of work, unless he has some pressing need or emergency at home.

➤ **Give your team an update on the team's/department's monthly performance report and goals.**

In such meetings, you will find suggestions coming from team members on how the targets can be met and you will find more involvement.

If an employee knows how his work has contributed to the organization, he will feel good about his work and will want to perform better. If the employee knows that his ideas can take the shape of results, it motivates him to think and contribute. More importantly, if the employee is a part of the discussion where he has a say in how targets can be achieved, he takes accountability to meet the target and gives his best, thereby encouraging others in the team to gun for the same. Team members start pushing each other to meet the target rather the team leader/manager pushing them daily.

➢ **Do a formal monthly feedback with your team members. Let them know what they have done well and where they need to improve on.**

Periodic feedback and support will help an employee look at his own performance and make necessary course correction to ensure that by the year end, he meets or exceeds his expected level of performance. Please ensure that you also provide them with help rather than just passing the buck by pointing their mistakes/weak areas. Let them know how you will monitor their progress and that you will be available for any support they may need.

➢ **Talk to them about their strengths and weakness with respect to their work and give them inputs as to how they can improve on their deliverables. If possible, help them by nominating for training or assigning a strong team member as their coach.**

Every employee likes to get enriched, add value to self in the form of training or acquiring additional skill sets. It is best when this is done at the workplace. It helps an employee understand his strengths and how to capitalize on them while at the same time identify his weakness that are deterrent to his work. At times, this exercise shows that a few team members can be more successful on other projects/teams rather than in their existing role/job or team.

➤ **Make a development plan for all your team members, which can be a part of the appraisal form and work on it along with the team member.**

The team member should be aware of his growth path in your team/organization and all possible growth avenues *(Could be in your team or in any other department through lateral movement)*. A Team Leader's success depends directly on the success of every team member in his team. If they perform well, you are more likely to get a better rating and if all of them are ready to move to the next level then you are sending a signal to your management that you are ready to move to the next level too.

➤ **Conduct a fair and unbiased appraisal in your team. The purpose of an appraisal system is not to make your team members happy but to reward them for their contribution, make them better at their jobs and help them grow by acquiring necessary skills. This can be done only if you conduct appraisals in a fair manner.**

Appraisals are a time when an employee gets to know what his contribution during the year has led to and how the organization values his contribution. An unbiased appraisal, though not in favour of the employee, will instil confidence in the employee about the organization's policies and fairness. On the other hand, if the employee finds the appraisal system unfair, firstly, he will not bother to perform up to expectations and secondly, he will go through the appraisal process as a mere formality and quit at the first opportunity.

Most employees confuse appraisals with promotion and this along with comparison of ratings with other team members becomes a major factor of dissonance. It is important to make employees understand that the appraisal is for their performance pertaining to the previous year (period) and promotion is based on competency and availability of position, based on the organization's policy.

At times, it is fine to let a team member feel bad if that is what his performance deserves.

➢ **Never make statements pointing to or branding a person's character. Instead, talk about your observation and give suggestions.**

It is always better to point to the behaviour and not the attitude or character of a person. Nobody likes anyone commenting on his or her character and if done, it will only lead to more negativity and the purpose of correcting the behaviour is lost. The moment a person senses that somebody is commenting on their attitude or personality, they shut themselves or listen only to respond/argue and not to understand. This defeats the purpose of the discussion. Give some examples of incidents, behaviour, and the outcome rather than point to it as an attitude issue.

> **All your team members deserve respect, irrespective of their potential, skill sets, performance, or any other factors.**

Everybody deserves respect, irrespective of their potential and performance. In an atmosphere of respect, people think positive and contribute better and in the absence of it they tend to think negative, behave negatively, and avoid working.

A team member can be a non-performer in one team, but he can be a star performer in another team/task and hence performance and skill set of a person should never decide how we treat an employee.

> **Put in place a training calendar for all your team members based on the performance appraisal feedback/discussion. Involve them while submitting the same to the HR team so that they understand the rationale of the nomination.**

Training helps the organization by shaping up the employees. It also helps employees become better professionals. Training is looked at as a major takeaway while searching for jobs or deciding to join an organization.

It is a major attraction and helps in employees making long-term career plans with the organization. The organization in turn can have their management team home grown, with a set of people who had joined at the starting level and scaled up based on training and performance in their roles. These people can become the role models for other employees.

➢ **Be honest with your team members, set realistic expectations, show genuine care for their feelings and career plans. Never promise them something that you cannot deliver. Be empathetic towards your team members.**

Trust and understanding are two major factors in people management and absence of these values will lead to unrest, de-motivation, and a higher rate of attrition. Always be sincere in setting expectations, committing to your team members and ensure that you put all your effort into making things happen as agreed upon.

➢ **Encourage them to participate in extra-curricular activities and be a part of as many activities as you can.**

Employees need to experience more than work in the organization. They should engage in activities to build and encourage team spirit. This is an informal way of getting people to work in a team and bond with each other. Build an informal/sports group within your team or a build a group from different teams so that they draw energy from each other, share ideas and develop a bond with each other.

➢ **Organize small events from time to time to break the monotony without disturbing work.**

On a periodic basis, if an organization has a small event, it breaks the monotony of work and re-energizes the team members. Having a social life at work is a welcome change for the employees and infuses positive energy in the team. There are instances where an employee finds it difficult to leave an organization due to the social life he enjoys in his current organization. The thought of letting it go and having to build a new one all over again holds him back.

➢ **Try to organize picnics or team movie outings on a quarterly basis, apart from the organization events. This will bring you closer to the team members and you will get to understand them better.**

Interacting with each other in an informal environment, getting to know each other on a personal level helps in building team spirit and creating better understanding among the team members. People relate to each other better if they interact in an informal gathering and develop a bond. This in turn strengthens the formal bond among team members and with the team leader. It makes the team leader/manager more approachable at work.

> ➤ **It is good to have a system to celebrate your team member's birthday by just gathering your team during lunch time or break period and cutting a cake. It is good to wish the team member as a team. If possible, the team can pool in money and buy a small gift for the team member. These small things matter the most when you expect a team member to consider the team as his family.**

This is a step towards valuing your team member as a person and making him feel a part of the family. Absence of this will not stop the work process but its presence will surely have a positive impact on the team. For the team member, this would mean that the organization wants to be a part of the employee's happiness and not just extract work from him.

> ➤ **Keep checking with your team members on how things are on the personal front. If you know of some problem at their end, ask if there is something you can do from the organization's side or personally to help him.**

It is important for the employee to feel that the organization wants to be a part of the employee's happiness and help him when he needs support in his personal life, to whatever extent the organization can help. This should not just be a formality but a sincere effort from the supervisor/manager to reach out and help his team members.

> ➢ **Demonstrate genuine respect for seniors when you introduce them to new employees.**

This conveys that, as a senior, an employee is valued and respected and this is an indirect message to a new employee to spend more time in the organization, to earn that respect from the organization. This also sets the expectation in the employee's mind that he also needs to respect his seniors as he experiences this during his initial days. One good practice followed by quite a few organizations in this regard, is to give away a Long Service Award to employees who have served in the organization for more than a certain period; this award is a certificate with a small token amount or gift coupon.

> ➢ **Last but not the least, an organization on its own is not a living entity but it is the people who run and manage the organization and give it a form – good, big, great, or bad.**

I think this is what all of us have experienced in our careers and would agree to.

We have covered how an employee decides to join an organization and settles in the organization and his team. Moving forward, we will try to understand how a Team Leader/Supervisor can get them to contribute and how he manages them.

Space to Make Notes for Readers

_____

_____

_____

_____

_____

_____

_____

_____

_____

_____

_____

_____

_____

_____

Why Build a Team When You Have Star Performers?

Often, we hear this statement about TEAM: **T**ogether **E**ach of us **A**chieve **M**ore. Let us try to get more details about why this is so.

The human body is the best example of teamwork. If we were to consider a human body as an organization/team and all the organs as team members, then understanding the necessity of teamwork becomes fun. For a body to remain healthy, perform well, all the organs need to contribute their best. No single organ can take overall charge. For instance:

- if the brain is working at its best and the heart is not working, then the body will collapse **(and)**

- if the heart is working at its best and the brain stops working, then the body will become a vegetable.

Similarly, in a team, all team members play an important role in their own way and unless and until all members contribute their best, the organization/team will not do well.

Even in the human body, based on the activity, certain organs play the lead role. (For example, when the body is doing a task related to thinking, the brain leads while all other organs support.) Similarly, certain team members may need to lead a task, based on their potential and capabilities and the task at hand.

All of us have some strengths and weaknesses. When one works in a team, it balances his strengths and weaknesses. In a team, everyone gives their best and get help from others on tasks they are not good at.

Individually, one can achieve targets, even exceed them, but that could be only for a single task. (Exception to this might be certain jobs where individual performance is a pre-requisite. For example, a programmer working single handedly on a project.) But in order to excel in all areas within his job description, he may need help and support from other team members. At a higher level, what one can accomplish as a team, he cannot do or will struggle to do individually.

A simple example to explain this point

Since most people in our country consider the game of cricket as their religion, let us understand team work in the context of cricket; In a match, if only Sachin Tendulkar scores a century and other team members do not score anything or score minimal and the bowlers fail to perform, then it is more likely that the team will lose the match, though Sachin Tendulkar's individual performance was exceptional. For a team to win, all players must contribute as per their strengths and only then the team stands a chance to win. Relying only on a single player is always a recipe for disaster.

In a team, all members learn from each other. They share knowledge and qualities with each other, and this enriches each one's personality. From an organization's point of view, a team is easier to drive than trying to drive individual team members. It consumes more management bandwidth and energy to get individuals to perform and in that context, teams are easier to drive, monitor and motivate. It is also a proven fact that teams are more dependable and reliable than high performing individuals.

As a team member, each one plays a vital role towards achieving the team goal and this makes them proud. Team players always have other team members to fill in for them, back them up and provide support as and when needed. Working in a team harnesses team spirit, feelings of ownership and belonging and this helps in building the organization.

More often, we find a tenured group of employees as a core team in an organization. This core team becomes the foundation on which the company's future is built. For all practical purposes, they will be the ones who will lay down the rules, policies, and values. All employees joining the company at a later stage will get trained by this core group and follow them.

In any organization, people will join and leave at some stage but with a team in place, the business runs as usual. This is one big advantage for the organization. The dependency on people moves on to processes and teams with shared responsibilities and goals.

Let Us Look at This Scenario

Alex was among the top three performers and whenever the team leader was running short on numbers he would bank on him. Alex would fill the gap and the team would meet its target. I was not very happy with this trend in the team and had warned the team leader on quite a few occasions that it was not an ideal way to work, where he banked on one team member. I wanted him to build the capability of his other team members.

On one occasion, when my team was chasing an aggressive target, this team member fell sick and could not make it to work for almost a week. That month, team failed to meet their target. This scenario is very common in teams, where the team or the team leader depends on individual performers to achieve team/ organization goals.

It is important for a Manager/Team Leader to understand that in one cricket team we cannot have 11 Sachin Tendulkars. Instead, we will have one such performer and other players with their own strengths. If it were possible to have 11 Tendulkars in one team, then our team would not need other batsmen. Since it is not possible and advisable to have a team full of Tendulkars, we need to have a combination of skill sets and somebody leading the team to plan and utilize the unique talent of the individuals effectively. In addition to this, having 11 Tendulkars would strengthen the team's batting but what would happen to the bowling, wicket keeping and fielding, because to complete a team you need to have all different skill sets in the team and not just one skill. Similarly, in organizations, teams cannot expect all exceptional performers, but we will have people with different skill sets, talent and that is why we have Team Leaders/ Assistant Managers/Managers to manage the resource pool effectively.

Another Incident

Rohit was an excellent performer in my team. The problem with him was that he would give his best and the results would be outstanding, but this would happen only if he decided to show up for work. Apparently, he was going through some personal issues and due to that he often took unscheduled leaves. This made him an unreliable resource. Now, if I as a manager, were to bank on him for the team goals to be met, then I would not be sure till the deadline if the team goal would be met. On the other hand, if I, as a Manager, depended on the entire team rather than an individual, my team goal is more likely to be met as I can always divide the gap between the target and actual achievement among other team members who'd fill in. How one handles such a team member is a different issue and we will see how this is done in another chapter.

For Team Leaders/Supervisors

It makes sense as an organization for us to make our employees work as a team rather than as individuals:

➢ **Individual performance helps a team and organization only in the short term. It is in the interest of the team, organization, to develop potential in your team rather than depending on individuals only.**

Banking on a pool of resources, rather than individuals is always an advantage. If the organization/Manager temporarily depends on an individual for a certain task, it is fine but that should not be a regular way of working or a long-term way of working. We have seen in the above-mentioned incidents, how dependency on individuals can lead to unpredictability and failures.

➤ **Ensure that your team is dependent on processes and not on individuals. Put in place process documents and implement the same in all your processes.**

It is better to depend on the team rather than on individuals. To take it a step further, it is better to have clearly defined processes and depend on them, rather than on the team members as individuals. Team members may change or leave but with the processes in place, the results are more likely to be consistent. This also helps in lowering the learning/training curve in the teams.

➤ **Gain the trust of your team members and trust them. This is the foundation of your team; without this you will not be able to build your team or work with them.**

If a team member does not trust his supervisor, most of his productive time will be spent in looking out for issues, talking about it, and worrying about them. Lack of trust in the supervisor or the organization will push the team member to spend more time on looking out for another job rather than contributing to the organization. As a supervisor / team leader, the first step of inculcating trust must be initiated by you. Do not expect your team or new joinees to trust you. You have to earn their trust by being sincere, genuinely caring for your team members and setting an example for them to follow.

➤ **Every team member is unique in terms of his capabilities, strengths. There is nothing like a perfect employee with all skill sets. It is also important to know that there cannot be another you. So be realistic and try to mix and match in your team based on their strengths and weaknesses.**

Relate to your team as your family. When in your own family, not all members understand and behave in a similar manner, even after spending a good amount of time together and having so many things in common, then how can you expect your team members to behave or/and perform in a similar manner? There are no readymade solutions. We must recruit employees for attitude. We can train, coach and nurture them to become an asset for the team/organization.

➤ **It makes the team leader's life easy; he does not have to provide help to every team member individually and he is not required to be there for everybody all the time.**

Team members help each other in the day-to-day work to ensure that the team goals are met. Dependency on the team and processes makes life easy for the supervisors and their focus shifts from being there to manage daily transactions to monitoring outputs, looking out for process optimization strategies and taking care of other critical responsibilities.

➢ **Most of the team leader's daily routine tasks which include ensuring that all the required people have come to work and no task is left unattended, are taken care of by the team and this enables him to focus on other important things.**

The advantage of shared responsibility and goals is that some things are done by the team without having to instruct. If the team has accepted the responsibility and is working on the goal, then all routine and minor things fall in place automatically and this happens due to team work and peer pressure. This helps the team leader to focus on creating learning opportunities for his team, making development plans and doing strategic thinking.

➢ **Working in a team provides motivation to all team members. This leads to a motivated and energetic team. Try to conduct team meetings and provide your team members with an opportunity to make suggestions.**

There are quite a few things one can do to motivate his team members. One thing in this regard, which is most critical, is to ensure your team members feel like they belong and give them a voice in your team. Motivation is directly related to energy and energy is directly related to better output.

➢ **Not all meetings can be conducted in a democratic manner where you seek participation from all team members. Sometimes, during crisis, one must**

conduct SLD *(Shut up, Listen and Do)* meetings, which means that the team leader has complete understanding of the situation and action is required immediately without wasting time in gathering opinions and suggestions.

A supervisor needs to always behave and conduct himself as per the need of the hour. In the absence of this, he will lose balance between people and the organization's goal. Sometimes, based on the need of the hour, speed of execution is to be given a higher priority and at other times, planning, gathering opinions and suggestions must be given priority. There is no one formula or one size fits all in managing teams. Different folks and different situations need different strokes.

➢ **Most people issues get resolved on their own in a team scenario. Encourage your team members to talk about the issues and settle it. If they are not able to do it by themselves, only then you get involved.**

When a team is working towards a common goal, then the forces within the team will not waste their time and energy on petty issues and will try to resolve things among themselves. It is advisable to not make the team dependent on you for every small situation or difference of opinion. Rather, give them space and methods they can adopt to resolve petty issues and small differences of opinion on their own.

➢ **Working in a team pushes a person to perform his best so that he is seen as a star/good performer in the team. On a periodic basis, announce the facts and figures of the best performers in your team meetings. This will ensure healthy competition and trigger peer pressure.**

Employees feel happy about their achievements when they have people around them who understand, celebrate their achievements and make them feel proud. Everybody craves for that recognition among their friends and family members and in a team, this feeling drives a person to work towards being an outstanding/star performer. Being recognized in front of your team for your performance, getting the congratulatory messages from the team and management is motivating for any team member.

➢ **Healthy competition among team members will make your team perform better.**

Competition, once triggered, is an ongoing motivation technique if it is kept healthy. Once team members start competing, then a supervisor has very little to do to drive his team to perform better. This will give him time to focus more on drafting and implementing attractive incentive schemes. A team member's achievement becomes significant when he has somebody to share his success with at work, where they understand the effort that was made and what that recognition means.

> ➤ **It is easy for the team leader to make development plans for his team members and put them in action. A strong team member will be able to coach the weaker members.**

With a team in place, a supervisor has a bigger and diversified resource pool available with him. In the absence of a team, either the supervisor must do all the coaching himself for all the team members or depend on external resources. In both cases, time and money is wasted. By giving opportunity to the better performing resources to coach new team members, it motivates the team members, since their performance gets noticed and they are given an opportunity to scale up.

> ➤ **With a good team in place, you get the confidence to accept challenges from management and this in turn paves the way for your growth.**

The team, with its combined skill sets, capabilities, and shared goals, gives confidence to the supervisor to accept projects and challenges given by the management. On one hand, this gives growth opportunity to the team leader and on the other, the team is recognized as a dynamic team, and gets the attention of management, budgets for learning and development. The team gets to learn new skills through the new projects and challenges accepted and executed.

> ➤ **By putting your team together, you are addressing the basic need of your team members and that is of being**

social. We all want to talk to somebody, have a friend at the workplace and this is the basic element of any team.

For team members, an organization/team is like a home away from home and this keeps them comfortable, positive, and enthusiastic at work. Sometimes, the only reason people want to come to work is because they look forward to spending time with their work friends or compete and get recognized by colleagues for their skills/performance.

➤ **Working in a team promotes the team members' willingness to change, to be adaptable, open-minded and to learn from others.**

We all learn from each other and the more we see others doing something good, the more we feel like learning and doing the same. It is the influence all of us have on each other when we interact with each other closely and work with each other. Sometimes, it can just be simple motivation. If my colleague can achieve it then I should also be able to achieve it. It makes difficult tasks/targets, relatable and achievable.

➤ **Working in teams is about shared goals and shared leadership. Allow team members to lead based on the key skills required for a project, so that you get the maximum out of your team members.**

This makes all team members feel that they play an important role in the team and their skill set and knowledge is respected and valued, they are given opportunity to demonstrate the same to the team. It also helps the team members learn how to lead others and align everybody with one goal.

> **There is no blame game in a team, all team members are equally responsible for the outcome. This in no way dilutes the Team Leader's overall responsibility for team goals.**

The basis of teamwork is shared responsibilities and goals. This means, if the team achieves, then all team members achieve and if the team fails then all team members fail. This will always keep them on their toes because a strong and performing team would never want to fail due to one mistake by any one team member. If the mistake happens, then the team will figure out course correction and implement it to avoid failing.

> **Last but not the least, most team leaders prefer to lead a strong and energetic team rather than a group of individual performers. It is not only in the interest of the organization or team, but also in the team leader's interest, to encourage and induce team spirit in all team members.**

Managing a group of people and driving them to one goal is a very challenging and exciting job. If one has an opportunity to do so, then one should not miss out on such a valuable and rich experience.

So, now we have the required team members, they are excited to be a part of the team and the organization. Let us now see what will make them excel at work.

Space to Make Notes for Readers

_____

_____

_____

_____

_____

_____

_____

_____

_____

_____

_____

_____

_____

_____

What Is in It for Me?

As mentioned earlier in the chapter 'What keeps them with you,' everybody has aspirations and goals in life and they constantly look for opportunities to fulfil them. This objective is the main driving force for a team member's performance and he always relates to the job or task based on, "What's in it for me?" If the task or job requires him to stretch in terms of work hours or efforts, this question becomes the deciding factor for the team member to accept the job/task. From the organization's context, it is very important for the team leader/manager to make this clear to all employees in both contexts: (a) employee's job/role (b) specific tasks.

Job/Role

Whenever an organization recruits a new employee or assigns a new role to an existing employee, the team leader/manager needs to explain to the team member about the expectations, rewards for the role and the career path in that function. From an organization's viewpoint, one needs to ensure that they have a clearly defined job description for every role in the company. The job description should necessarily have details like:

- Role name

- Description and key responsibilities

- Level or band of the role

- Reporting to position

- Educational qualification required

- Additional qualification required (if any)

- Experience (details about the number of years and stream/industry)

- Incentives and rewards

While all this is good for a person to match his profile to the job description, it would be good, if one can add a few more points to be given to the employee. *(This should be given only at the stage where the offer is being made. It need not be for public consumption):*

- Specify and give details about the next two levels above the said position.

- Elaborate on the pre-requisites like number of years of experience required in the previous position, previous performance ratings and any additional skill sets, or qualifications required.

- Number of years the employee must serve in the organization to be eligible to move to the next level.

This information helps the prospective employee match the organization hierarchy and growth opportunities with his own career plans and take the right decision. If an employee accepts the offer after getting a clear understanding of the job description and growth opportunities, then his chances of staying in the organization and performing up to his potential are higher.

During the induction period, clarity among all the new employees regarding their understanding of the role and job description, must be checked. Resolve their queries and doubts and if there is any disconnect, clarifying to employees at this stage would prevent early attrition. Giving the employees an overall view of the organization plans and linking it to their specific function targets would help them get a sense of how important their role is and the impact it has on the overall organization goals.

Further, narrowing it down to their specific team and individual targets, helps them understand what is in store for them in terms of learning, money, and growth prospects due to business expansion or better perks and facilities in the near future.

Specific Tasks

One common comment from team members in most organizations is, "Why me....why have I been selected for this task?" or "This is not a part of my key deliverables." All these comments mean one thing: "What's in it for me?" As human beings, we tend to check for returns based on our contribution and there is nothing wrong, inappropriate or selfish about it. In fact, it is good if employees feel this way or ask these questions because the fact that their mind is filled with these questions means that they are looking for some positive indications to perform at work, they are serious about working in the organization and want to get the best returns. This also indicates that the employee is not there to waste his time and in turn the organization's time.

When a Team Leader/Supervisor has additional projects on hand other than the regular deliverables, he looks out for a capable and reliable resource in the team to take on the additional task and execute the project. The challenge is to get the project done by a resource whose key deliverables do not include such a project. On one hand, the team leader is confident about the competency of the identified team member but on the other, he has the challenge of getting the identified resource to accept it, as it is not a part of his key deliverables.

This is a common scenario and from an organization's point of view one can:

- Have a provision in the performance appraisal system to recognize and reward such ad-hoc projects executed by team members.

- It would be great if the team leader could account for it in the promotion policy by giving some weightage to the additional projects worked on by team members.

- If in any case, one cannot go to the extent of changing/ incorporating efforts put into ad-hoc projects, then this should be linked to the periodic reward/award system.

Unless one of the above options is on the table, getting any additional projects executed will always be a challenge in the long run. The exception to this rule is one scenario where a team member is being sent for some training program which would help him acquire additional skill sets so that he can execute the project to the required standards. In such cases, the team member looks at the training as a big return for stretching himself for the project.

One more common problem is a team member who says, "If you want me to do this, I will do it" or "If you think this will be good for me, then I will do it." This simply means that at times, the team member puts too much trust in his immediate boss or manager and leaves the decision to him. The only thing that keeps them going is the fact that the team leader/manager will make them do something which is going to benefit them. The perceived benefit could be learning, an opportunity to show their talent, prove their capability and this can lead to growth. The onus of thinking good and taking a decision in such a scenario shifts from the team member to the team leader/manager.

Let Us Look at an Example

I got a requirement from another department for a team member with analytical skills and the role was critical. I had a fair idea of the potential of my team members, their previous work experience and career aspirations. I chose one team member who would be perfect to move from my department to the other department. This team member had skills and experience relevant to the other function and he was the best choice.

I called the team member for a meeting to discuss the opportunity in the other team and asked his opinion about moving. The team member, more than anything else, wanted to understand the rationale of how he was identified for the role. I explained about the new role, how relevant his previous experience would be and how his skills could be put to use in the new role. The team member responded, "You know my potential and the work I have put in here and I think you know what is best for me."

For Team Leaders/Supervisors

It is a common scenario for a team leader to come across team members, who either do not understand the role/

career path clearly or have complaints about the same not being communicated clearly or correctly. This leads to de-motivation and subsequently, resignation. When an employee goes through this sort of experience, he loses trust in the organization, loses interest in the job and his focus shifts to finding alternate jobs and roles to fulfil his career goals.

Rahul was a new team member in my team who resigned during the initial training period itself. While accepting his resignation, I enquired with him on the reason for resigning and the details that came out of the discussion were quite shocking: One of his friends worked with our organization in another department; the department was a specialized function and had specific requirements pertaining to qualification, skill set and experience. Rahul expressed to his friend about his desire to work for this department. His friend advised Rahul to join my team and later move to the desired department through internal job posting or lateral transfer. He had decided to join, thinking about moving to the specialized department internally. During the induction period, all the new employees were informed that movement into the specialized function was not possible unless the eligibility criteria was met. Rahul realized that he would not be able to work in the specialized function, which he was interested in and hence he decided to resign.

In this case, there was miscommunication on the part of the organization, though not by HR but by one of the existing employees, who either, did not have a very clear understanding of the internal process, or assumed that the internal procedures could be manipulated.

There are two steps in dealing with such situations:

1. The first step in handling such cases is to investigate and analyze where and how the miscommunication happened and then look out for a solution. Once it is established that miscommunication did happen from the organization's side or an employee has misunderstood the role, then the team leader needs to explore the possibility of accommodating the team member in any other function, where his career goals could be met.

2. If the team leader is not able to find an option for the team member within the organization, then he needs to communicate this clearly to the team member and inform him of what he could possibly achieve by being with the organization. At this point, if the team member expresses his desire to leave due to this reason, the team leader and the organization needs to respect the decision and ensure that the team member's exit is smooth.

While we are on this topic, let me share my thoughts on something I consider very important. Many management personnel have this misconception that an employee's entry into the organization should be very smooth so that he feels good about joining the organization and gives his best. I strongly feel that along with smooth entry, it is very important for an employee to have a very smooth exit too. In the long run, an employee always talks highly about his previous employer and this becomes a big attraction for others who may be looking for a change. A sincere, good, and proud ex-employee is a much better soundboard for the organization than an existing employee bad mouthing the organization.

Some tips on how to identify and assign an ad-hoc project to a team member:

1. Make a list of team members who you feel can execute the project in the best possible manner. It is always better to have more than one person identified and if you are not able to find more than one, it surely indicates that you have some work on hand as Team Leader/Supervisor to build your team's skill levels.

2. Sit with the identified team members on a one-on-one discussion and explain the project, the desired knowledge and skill level required to execute the project. Based on the discussion, finalize the best of them in terms of enthusiasm and capability.

3. Explain to the other team members, who have not been assigned the project, the criteria for finalizing the team member. Provide them with feedback. Let them know if they need to improve on something so that they can work on additional projects in future.

4. Reward them (If you have provision for this in your organization):

- Monthly reward program

- Add some weightage in their annual appraisal

- Consider this point when finalizing the promotion list (*Please do not make this the sole reason for promoting a person.*)

Based on the significance of the project, you can use one of the options mentioned above to reward the team member.

It is very important for the team leader to be fair while selecting a team member for a project and suitably reward him so that in future, you will have more team members coming forward for additional projects.

➢ **Do monthly feedbacks with your team members.**

The feedback process makes things clear to team members on where they stand. At the same time, it makes your work easy during annual appraisals. If you conduct monthly feedbacks for your team members, then annual appraisals involve just summing up the monthly feedback. Monthly feedbacks are a proactive approach to help and facilitate team members meet their targets. It also provides an opportunity for team members to do course correction and meet their KRAs at the end of the year.

➤ **Put in place a career plan for your team members based on their potential, experience, performance and communicate the same to them. Break down the career plan into milestones and periodically review them with the team members.**

It is very important for team members to feel that the supervisor and the organization are concerned about their career plan and growth. Once the employee gets this confidence, he can visualize his growth in the organization and would want to give his best.

The plan needs to have a summary of where the team member stands as on date and the skills he needs to acquire by a certain period. In case a team member is expected to gain some experience in a specific task/project, then timelines for the same should be specified with expected level of output/outcome. There should be no room left for any ambiguity.

➤ **Timely recognition for good work is important. The recognition could be a big award, promotion or just a pat on the back. Ensure that your team members get the deserved credit and recognition for their good work.**

None of us would want to contribute without the knowledge of what our contributions would lead to in terms of recognition, reward, or growth. Recognition is a pat on the back for the good work done by the employee and as an organization it conveys the message: "We know your contribution and we value it." It is very important to not delay the reward. A small reward or some form of appreciation should be immediately rolled out. Delayed recognition can sometimes de-motivate the team member.

➢ **It is good practice for an organization to follow a performance-based incentive and growth approach. But it is more important to put this in practice by communicating the key deliverables, expectations and achievements with facts and figures.**

Communication is the most important factor to build trust in your team members. If an employee is not aware of the key deliverables and the performance rating factors, then it would not be possible for him to deliver results as expected. When the key deliverables are handed over in writing, then it commits an employee to the expected output. In the absence of this, there will always be animosity in the team and a feeling of unfairness.

➢ **When you are in a situation where you must get additional work/projects done, always look out for a win-win solution and guard the interests of your team members while getting the work done.**

The simpler situation would be that the organization policy permits the team leader to announce rewards and returns for accepting and delivering the additional project. In the absence of this, if an employee has the confidence in his supervisor about his interests being protected, he would be willing to take up additional projects or tasks assigned to him. This confidence is built over a period by observing how others are dealt with and his own previous experience with the supervisor.

➢ **Whenever you have to give any advice to your team members, remember that your team members have put their trust in you and you need to offer them an unbiased, fair opinion and give them all the information that can be shared with them.**

It is very important that team members look up to their supervisor, trust him so that they value his feedback, advice and accept the same. If the advice is about a team member's personal situation and as a team leader, you feel that you are not competent or not sure of what advice to give him, then it is important that you convey the same to the team member and direct him to a competent source. If possible, arrange that meeting and discussion. If the advice being sought by the team member is on the professional front, then your advice must be very sincere and unbiased, even if it hurts the team or organization in the short run.

➢ **Build potential in your team members by giving them inputs, sharing knowledge, and nominating them for necessary trainings.**

For an employee, this is the only positive factor besides money. While sharing your knowledge, be conscious that you do not use big jargons. Talk to them in simple language. Absence of training may not harm the organization in the short run but following this practice will certainly benefit the organization in the long run because the organization is putting in efforts to make their employees better professionals by imparting valuable knowledge. The training calendar for employees is a major attraction when candidates are looking/applying for a job in an organization.

➢ **Always look out for opportunities to enrich your team members. Share with them good readings, books, or articles. This can be done on a one-on-one basis or in team meetings.**

Sharing need not always be in the form of a lecture or books. It could be a simple presentation, a good article, or a simple WhatsApp forward related to a subject which provides learning for team members. It can be some new insight or additional knowledge pertaining to their area of work or related to their sector which will help them in performing better or give new direction to their career. Sometimes, it can be a simple, new and interesting bit of news/knowledge with no direct relation to their job.

Refer to the example below which you will find in most organizations

Vikas joined an organization as a manager. He had no experience in managing people but got this job due to his performance in his previous organization and his good relations with the CEO of the new organization. His experience was only technically relevant to his current role. Now, he had a challenge to take over this position and prove his worth. Vikas started reading management books and spoke to his other friends who were in people management roles and took their advice – this was a good thing to do.

What did not work in his favour was that he presented his knowledge acquired from his friends and management books as his own concepts, ideas and lectured his team during team meetings. Sometimes, the team members failed to understand the concepts due to the use of heavy jargons. At the same time, Vikas was not able to explain details of what he had presented, due to lack of understanding on his part. A few team members were very impressed with Vikas initially. However, soon they realized that the concepts and ideas were not his own but taken from management books. The mistake that Vikas made was firstly, he tried to present other people's ideas as his own.

Secondly, he tried to impress his team members by using jargon, talking about things he did not have complete understanding of and hence struggled to explain them properly. Due to this, he lost the trust and respect of his team members. This made his team very cautious and observant. They noticed that on quite a few occasions, Vikas would credit himself for his team member's ideas.

We have seen how and why employees join an organization, what keeps them with the organization, how the team culture helps them and what their expectations are. Let us now look at the subtle factors that draws an employee towards an organization and retains them.

Space to make notes for readers

_____

_____

_____

_____

_____

_____

_____

_____

_____

_____

_____

_____

_____

_____

Does Somebody Care for Me?

Care, or employee care, has become a fashion statement in today's corporate world. Today, all organizations boast of employee care but miss out on basics. The following questions determine the genuineness of any tall claims made about employee care by an organization:

1. Does the organization have only good policy documents, or do they have good practices as well?

2. Does the organization encourage employees to talk about their issues, concerns, and ideas?

3. Does the organization provide employees with more than one platform to get answers to their questions and raise their issues?

4. Does somebody in the organization get back to the employees with an answer or solution and do they have a mechanism in place to monitor the same?

5. Does the organization make employees feel wanted and important or are they busy chanting, "Customer

comes first," and in the process end up neglecting the employees?

6. Do the employees like and look forward to coming to work?

7. Do the employees enjoy their work or just wait for pay day?

8. Are the employees happy to be a part of the organization?

9. Does the organization make any effort to check if employee expectations are understood and met?

10. Does the organization help the employees grow not only unilaterally but overall, as professionals, so that they can find their own way in the outside, competitive, corporate world?

11. Is the organization competitive in terms of paying its employees?

12. Is the organization sensitive to employee needs and concerns?

13. Does the company have a clearly defined POSH policy and committee?

14. Does the organization encourage employees to have friends in the workplace?

15. Does the organization give the employees ample opportunities to socialize by having team/company get-togethers?

16. Does the organization involve the employee's family by asking them to visit the premises or inviting them for team/company parties?

When an organization hires a new employee, they hire more than just the skill set and experience. They hire a total personality who has some social, economic, financial, and emotional needs along with qualifications, experience and skill sets. Human beings, by nature, are social beings with emotional needs and emotional intelligence. Very often, these points are ignored by most organizations. They appoint employees for their experience, qualification, skill sets and expect good results by just giving them work tools.

By providing work tools, the organization is just taking care of the necessity for an employee to work. What makes an employee perform his best and feel a part of the organizational family?

Few, if not all the above-mentioned questions will be answered in the following pages.

Given below are a few possible solutions/answers to the questions raised above:

➤ **Does the organization have only good policy documents, or do they have good practices as well?**

Making good, employee friendly policies is one thing but implementing them is totally different. Apart from implementing the policies, the organization needs to go beyond policies and ensure it results in employees considering themselves an important part of the organization. They should feel like the workplace is their second home.

Orientation programs should be conducted for all people in managerial roles so that they develop sensitivity towards their team members and other employees. The culture of the company should revolve around employee care and it will be helpful if this factor reflects in the Vision and Mission statement of the company.

➤ **Does the organization encourage employees to talk about their issues, concerns and ideas?**

This must be promoted in all company forums and by all management team members on a regular basis. This needs to be drilled down right from the induction to the exit interview.

A **POSH committee** is a mandatory requirement for all organizations that have more than a certain number of employees, so that female employees feel safe and have forums/committees to approach if they face any sexual harassment in the workplace.

A **360-degree feedback** is the best mechanism to encourage employees to express their opinion and provide valuable feedback on their higher ups or any other issues at work. **Organization Health Survey** is a very good mechanism to provide insight into employee morale and other issues.

Some organizations undermine the importance of this, but it proves very beneficial in the long run to have this done by the experts in the market. Unfortunately, most organizations do not take this up due to:

1. Cost.

2. Hassle of getting an external agency. Coordinating and managing this activity becomes a big task.

3. Reluctance in involving a third party that will get information about the weaknesses of the organization.

The above-mentioned reasons are valid. The possible alternative would be to run this activity on a yearly basis through the internal HR team but in a fair manner, where all information and feedback from an employee is kept confidential. The knowledge required to run this survey can be acquired by getting one of the HR resources trained, who can subsequently share the learning and knowledge with other HR team members. This proves helpful in the long run.

As an organization, we sometimes fail to recognize the value of our human resources. These resources understand our business. They are an integral part of service/product delivery and play a major role in customer experience. While we are willing to pay an external organization/ consultant to come and tell us what we can do better or how we can improve our products and services, we do not seek feedback and suggestions from our own employees on the same. Taking ideas from our team members helps in the following ways:

1. It gives them pride to contribute and see their idea come to life.

2. It cuts down cost which we would otherwise incur in getting an external firm/consultancy to do the job.

3. It motivates team members and can be used as a tool to reward and retain employees.

4. It utilizes the vast resource pool and creates the possibility for fresh ideas.

Two of the organizations I was associated with in the past followed different methodologies to encourage employees to send in their ideas and suggestions:

In one organization, they placed a suggestion/idea box in every department, where employees could drop in their suggestions and ideas and the box would be checked once a week. The ideas and suggestions would be thoroughly analyzed for feasibility and then implemented/rejected and communicated back to the employee via mail. If an employee's idea was accepted and implemented, then he would be suitably rewarded in the company-wide meeting.

In the other organization, the company had created a mail ID for employees to send their suggestions and had also provided employees with an internal blog to post their suggestions. The mail ID and blog were checked by all the function heads for suggestions relevant to their functions and analyzed for feasibility and then implemented/rejected. There was an award for maximum number of suggestions given by an employee and based on the implementation/impact of the suggestion, an employee would be awarded.

Skip Meetings By Managers and Functional Heads

The purpose of this meeting is to give employees a platform where they can voice their discomfort, discuss issues they face in their team with their team members, Managers and other teams and bring it to the notice of the Management for resolution. This ensures that there are checks and balances in the organization. Everybody is aligned and working towards the company's objectives and the business is not being run as per a Manager's personal agenda and goals. This should not be made a platform for people to create issues for their Managers to settle personal scores. This exercise should be done very objectively, fairly and any element of subjectivity and bias should be removed so that the purpose is not diluted.

HR Meetings/One-on-One Meetings

This should be done in a manner that the employees are encouraged to raise proper issues. Filtering needs to be done or else this can become a tool to level scores with each other. It can lead to employees being forced and provoked to raise issues which do not exist.

➢ **Does the organization provide employees with more than one platform to get answers to their questions and raise their issues?**

Employees need to be given more than one forum where they can talk about their issues, concerns and grievances. There are different approaches adopted by different organizations.

- Some organizations have a group ID where issues and queries can be sent by the team members. This mail is received by the head of the function and HR head. (Some organizations have employees at the management level nominated for such tasks). Employee details are kept confidential and action is taken on the issue, if found genuine.

- Some organizations have boxes placed in all departments where an employee can write about his issue/concern and drop it in the box. The same is checked and actioned by a selected group of people on a daily/weekly basis. Again, confidentiality is maintained about the employee.

- Few organizations put the Open-Door policy in practice by putting in place an escalation matrix, where in they define various levels starting from the Team Leader right up to the CEO for employee redressals.

- Some organizations provide an employee with an option to post his issue or grievance on the intranet site and this in turn is acted upon by the appointed committee. The employee gets an answer from an identified person from the committee in the form of an email explaining the action taken.

➢ **Does somebody in the organization get back to the employees with an answer or solution and do they have a mechanism in place to monitor the same?**

More important than putting this mechanism in place is the timely outcome. The employee feels confident only when he gets to know that such issues are taken up and addressed within a specified time and it is done fairly.

➤ **Does the organization make the employees feel wanted and important or are they busy chanting, "Customer comes first," and in the process neglecting the employees?**

Make employee care a part of your organization/team culture and let it reflect in every gesture. Employee care needs to find a place in the Vision and Mission statement of the company. An organization will not have employees giving their best to customers, if they do not feel they are getting the best treatment and care.

For an employee to do his job with enthusiasm and energy, he needs to feel important and happy. Only then he will pass on this feeling to customers. A de-motivated employee can never sound cheerful or give his best to the organization or to customers. In today's context, the employee comes first and only then customers. If the organization does not have employees, then who will bring the customers and who will be there to serve them?

➤ **Do the employees like and look forward to coming to work?**

If an employee finds his workplace as his second home then he will look forward to coming to work daily. This is possible only:

- If he has friends in the organization
- He feels that he can achieve more than just career goals

- He is adding value to himself as a professional and as a person

- Trusts the management

- Feels happy and proud to be a part of the organization

- Feels his career and economic needs will be fulfilled by the organization and his contribution is valued.

➢ **Do employees enjoy their work or just wait for pay day?**

Salary becomes incidental, if all the above-mentioned parameters are worked on and the employee feels proud to be a part of the organization. Money is important for all of us but if that becomes the sole reason for coming to work, then it speaks volumes about employee morale. If this is something that is common to all or most employees in an organization, then it speaks about the culture of the organization. Employees should look forward to coming to work due to the energy, fun filled culture where they get to learn, compete with their colleagues and give shape to their career plans.

➢ **Are the employees happy to be a part of the organization?**

Organization Health Survey is the best indicator. Apart from this, the attrition rate, or average tenure of employees in the organization, absenteeism rate and performance level of employees is a good indicator. An organization's year on year growth percentage along with the attrition rate trend is a good indicator of the employee's happiness index.

> **Does the organization make any effort to check if employee expectations are understood and met?**

In this direction, the organization needs to invest time and money in conducting skip meetings and Organization Health Surveys. All the outcomes of Skip meetings and One-on-One meetings will serve as a reality check and present the true picture of the employees' opinion. Any outcome/suggestions that come because of the skip meeting and Organization Health Survey should be taken up seriously for implementation. Else, it will lose its meaning. Action is needed to demonstrate the seriousness of this exercise to the employees.

> **Does the organization help employees grow not only unilaterally but overall, as professionals, so that they can find their own way in the outside, competitive corporate world?**

Employee growth and development plans are very important. It is important to ensure that the organization has a proper training calendar for all employees. In the performance appraisal system, more importance should be given to the areas of development of an employee. Put together an action plan and monitor it closely and periodically.

Training on latest tools and technology in their work area needs to be imparted on a regular basis. When an employee leaves the organization, he needs to carry all good values and learning from the organization. This in no way means that the organization trains people for the outside world. Instead, doing this attracts the best talent and helps in retaining well trained employees who are excellent performers.

➤ **Is the organization competitive in terms of paying its employees?**

It is a good practice to conduct market survey at least on an annual basis and make market correction a part of the annual salary hike. Failing to do this will lead to losing good performers to competition while poor performers remain in the system.

➤ **Is the organization sensitive to employee needs and concerns?**

Empathy is the secret. This must reflect in each gesture of the supervisory and management team members. Proper and timely action on issues raised is important to infuse trust in employees and make them feel valued. The organization must communicate to employees how important and valuable their feedback is and how it will help the organization make it a better workplace.

> **Does the organization encourage employees to have friends in the workplace?**

As a social being, all of us like to talk to others, share our feelings/problems with others and this is a big emotional outlet. If this part is missing, an employee comes to work out of compulsion, with his fears and anxiety and this hampers work. A friend is an answer and guiding force that motivates an employee to look forward to coming to work. Once they are at work, bonding with others, sharing, competition, perks and growth opportunities push a person to perform at his best, so that he will be looked up to by his friends and other co-workers.

> **Does the organization give employees enough occasion to socialize by having get-togethers?**

All work and no fun makes an employee a dull employee. It is important for the organization to provide employees with enough opportunities to socialize, celebrate, relax, have fun in an informal environment so that it re-energizes them to give their best. This also provides them with an opportunity to interact with employees in other functional areas and management team members in an informal manner. They start associating themselves with others and draw inspiration to do better. The best opportunity is the company-wide awards and rewards ceremonies and team outings.

> ➤ **Does the organization involve the employee's family by asking them to visit the premises or inviting them for team/company parties?**

Providing the employees an opportunity on a regular basis to make their families a part of organization events, or just to visit their workplace induces a feeling of pride and belonging in them. They like to show off to their family members their work area, company premises, the facilities and the boss's cabin (which they aspire to occupy one day). They are keen to show their families how important they are in the organization.

It is very important for employees to feel that they are treated as human beings and they are not just a means to achieving organizational goals. They need to feel that they are a part of the organizational family; this keeps the organization in good health.

It is of utmost importance for employees to feel that the organization and especially the management team is there to provide any help and guidance that they may require from time to time.

For Team Leaders/Supervisors

Everything a Team Leader does or does not do, influences the employee's morale and career plans.

> **As a team leader, one needs to be always approachable and cheerful. This sets the work environment and culture in the team.**

It is a big comfort factor for the team member that he can approach his team leader/manager whenever he needs help, information, or support. A team leader or a manager is there for his team and he should never be busy when they need him. He must remain approachable and welcome them to approach him whenever they need to speak to him. If an employee finds his supervisor a gloomy and serious or negative person, then he would avoid all possible contact with him, all the time. On the other hand, if he finds his supervisor a positive and cheerful person, he will look for every small opportunity to talk to the supervisor as that induces positivity and cheerfulness in him.

> **It is an age-old practice; the team leaders get pressure from top and they pass it on to their team members directly. A team leader needs to absorb the pressure and pass on just the tasks related to the pressure and not the pressure itself.**

A team leader/supervisor needs to function like a shock absorber for the team. He needs to understand that it is his job to get work done by his team and be accountable for the collective performance of his team. When he starts passing the pressure on to his team directly, then his role is in question.

Further, the role of a Supervisor is to break the big picture into small tasks to be executed by the team. The team may not be able to understand the implications of their mistakes/failures and it is the Supervisor's job to translate and explain it in a way that makes sense to the team. Passing on the pressure blindly will confuse and scare the team.

> **As a team leader, one needs to know that he cannot give everything that the team members want but he can make them feel important and a valued part of the team. This is possible by caring for them, coaching them and helping them perform better.**

Being there all the time for his team is a basic expectation from a team leader/supervisor. This is not in the literal or physical sense, but whenever a team member is struggling or needs help, a supervisor must do the best he can in that situation to assist and support his team member. The team member needs to have the confidence that his supervisor is always there to help and support him in doing his job better. Though the relationship starts between a supervisor and a team member purely at a professional level, over a period of time, a bond develops between them which results in dependency, both in professional and personal aspects of life. A good supervisor is like a father figure, elder member of the family, whom the team looks up to and expects support in times of need.

➤ **The team member needs to be assured that his personal matters and issues are kept confidential by the team leader and that by raising issues or by putting forward his grievance, he will not be reprimanded.**

This point is very often ignored and leads to employees losing trust in their supervisor/organization. It becomes worse when they stop speaking. When an employee stops speaking about his problems and issues to the supervisor/organization, then on one hand it deprives the supervisor/organization of an opportunity to make corrections and on the other, the employee starts speaking about these issues to outsiders. When this happens, we come across a situation where the team leader is not aware of the issues in his team/organization, but the outside world is aware of it and is probably getting ready to take advantage of the situation.

➤ **Be sensitive and emphatic to your team member's needs, feelings and aspirations. Most importantly, never make fun of any team member's opinion, suggestion or ideas even if it sounds silly or simple.**

First, our team members are human beings, then employees and as human beings they want to share. They expect the organization to take care of them. Let us not forget, great inventions/ideas were often ridiculed by people initially.

A supervisor needs to encourage his team members to speak their mind so that all team members think and contribute to the betterment of the organization.

If a team member fears that his ideas will not be taken seriously and will be made fun of, then they will never put forward their ideas. This can be a big loss for the organization because people who are on the front end dealing with customers, understand their pulse, service and product areas of improvements far better than others who do not interact with customers on a daily basis. These valuable inputs and suggestions from the team can help the organization in getting ahead of competition and in staying ahead of the curve.

> **Respect your team members for what they are as individuals. Never try to intimidate them.**

Respect for all and respect for their opinions and feelings is important in our personal lives too. If the supervisor does not respect his team members, he cannot expect the team members to respect him, though he is a level above them in the hierarchy. The team members should feel comfortable talking to their team leader and must not fear approaching him.

Any supervisor who uses his hierarchical position to get team members to listen to him is likely to be only feared but not necessarily respected. To get respect from the team, the supervisor must genuinely respect each team member. Respect is gained only by being true, imparting knowledge, supporting and caring for others genuinely.

➢ **Avoid using management concepts or jargon. Talk to your team members in simple language which is understood by them.**

The idea of communicating with the team members is to teach them and this is not possible if we speak in a way they would not be able to understand. Whenever a team leader/supervisor is speaking to his team members, either individually or in a meeting, it is important that he gets down to their level and speaks at that level so that the message is conveyed effectively. There is no point in trying to impress your team members by using jargon to show off your knowledge, because they will not be able to understand. Instead, it is always better to talk to them with the intention to make them understand and improve rather than just to impress.

➢ **Keep things straight and simple as far as you can and do not give vague answers/justifications.**

For team members, the team leader/supervisor is the organization. If they do not get clear answers, they begin to suspect all the information passed on to them. This is very crucial to help team members build trust in their team leader and the organization. It also helps avoid the suspicions and fears of team members which may build due to lack of information or ambiguity. If team members believe that their supervisor speaks his mind and is always straightforward, then they are less likely to waste time in gossip or trying to get information elsewhere. It also helps in setting clear expectations for team members.

➢ **Accept your mistakes if you feel you are wrong. Take steps to correct yourself. There is nothing bad about being wrong. It is human to be wrong at times.**

By accepting mistakes, a team leader/supervisor displays how responsible and humble he is. This sends a signal to team members to replicate this behaviour. Mistakes are committed only by people who intend to do something and not by people who just sit around without putting in any effort. It is important to make the team understand that making mistakes is acceptable but trying to hide them under the carpet, blaming others or repeating the same mistake is not acceptable. By accepting his mistakes, the supervisor is leading by example rather than avoiding responsibility.

➢ **Work with them and be a facilitator rather than becoming a boss or trying to make them work for you.**

Respect and not fear should be the driving force; the team member should contribute willingly in an atmosphere of trust and respect. An atmosphere of strict line of hierarchy and directives instils fear and in such an atmosphere, the level of contribution and creativity is not optimal. Shared goals rather than top-down instruction is a preferable approach. A supervisor is an enabler. His role is to debug and clear obstacles for his team members, get them the necessary information and tools to complete their job. Merely giving instructions will not get the desired results or at least not at the expected level always.

➤   **Encourage and accept that your team members will make mistakes.**

Let them know that it is okay if mistakes happen while trying to do something rather than not trying to do anything. Needless to say, ensure that they learn from their mistakes and they do not repeat the same. It would help the team members, if the supervisor sits with them and makes them understand the implications of the mistake, provides them with support and guidance on how to carry on with their work without committing the same mistake. A work environment where mistakes are not used to crucify employees, encourages them to think out of the box, ideate and innovate, which is a very positive and healthy sign for the organization.

➤   **Never ever give your team members a feeling that you are too busy to listen to them or to talk to them when they approach you.**

A team leader/supervisor's main responsibility is to manage his team, take care of them, play the role of an enabler and if one is not able to spare time to talk to them, then team members will not expect much from him. The team member gets a feeling that he is not an important part of the team and distances himself from the team leader/supervisor. This shows how empathetic a supervisor is about his team members.

A team leader/manager's job is to ensure that he is always available for his team, to help and support them to make their job easy. Any other job for a team leader/manager is secondary when his team needs to talk to him or needs his time/support and this should be non-negotiable.

> **If you care for your team members, care for them genuinely or else just do not fake it or talk about it because pretensions in this aspect can only be damaging.**

Care for team members must be genuine and heartfelt. If you genuinely feel it, it shows in every word you speak and in everything you do. Pretensions make a team member lose trust in the team leader/organization.

I was working with a company as an Assistant Manager. I had this habit of greeting all my team members when I walked into my office each morning. One day, when one of my team leaders was giving feedback to a team member, the team member got emotional and burst out that she felt nobody in the team liked her. She felt left out of the team and due to this her concentration was impaired. When the Team Leader probed further, the team member expressed that apart from the petty differences she had with a few other team members, the manager did not greet her when he walked past her workspace. This made her feel that she was disliked and not wanted in the team.

Now, if you look at the issue from my point of view, it was very simple. This team member's desk was at the entrance of the department, with her back towards the door. During those days, I was pre-occupied with team appraisals and team re-structuring, I used to rush past the door to my desk, without stopping at that team member's desk to greet her and have the usual chat. At the same time, my other team members would see me coming and they would greet me, and I would greet them back. Little did I realize that such a small thing could be so important to that team member.

Keeping this incident in mind, if we are serious about employee care, then we should not just think of having employee oriented/friendly policies, but it should reflect in every behaviour of ours.

Another Example

One of my team members got sick. I asked the Team Leader (immediate boss) to go to the team member's house and check if he needs any help and assistance. (This team member had relocated from another city and was staying in a bachelor accommodation). The Team Leader visited the team member, took him to the doctor as he was very weak to go on his own, bought medicines, something to eat and dropped him back to his place. For the next two to three days, the Team Leader and I used to call this team member and check on his health. This team member was so touched that even after about a year, he continued to talk about this to other team members. After he left the organization, he kept in touch with us. He continued to talk about this in his new company to his team members.

Employee welfare policies are just the beginning towards employee care and not the end. One may do everything as per the company policy and still team members may end up saying, "Nobody cares for me in this company." This is because we need to genuinely feel and care for our team members as human beings, as family members and not restrict ourselves to policies. Something that we consider to be a small gesture can be quite a big comfort for team members.

One More Example

One team member in my team had left the organization and relocated to another city. She was due to receive a signed Provident Fund form from the company which did not reach her. Despite her repeated interactions for more than a month, with HR and Finance department, her problem remained unresolved. As a last resort, she called me to help her resolve the issue. I took all the details from her and assured her of resolving the problem. I personally contacted the HR dept and followed up with them for two days. On the third day her issue was resolved, and I communicated this to her personally.

When you genuinely care for team members, do it at all times. It does not matter if they are good or average performers or if they presently work with you or have left the organization. Build that kind of trust and faith in them so that they will be sure they can always look up to you and reach out to you. If within your capacity you can do something small, it may mean everything for them so just do it. You may not even have to put in much effort and time into it, but it goes a long way in building the reputation of the organization and improving your own image in the organization and in the industry.

Now in this case if you look at it from the manager's point of view:

I had about more than 100 people in my team and there would have been quite a few who would have left the organization. I could have just sent an email to HR with the details given to me by the ex-team member and forgotten about it. There was no need for me to put in additional effort and energy on an issue which an ex-employee had with the organization. But, if you genuinely care for your team members then it doesn't matter if they are good performers or average performers, or if they are currently working with you or they had worked with you in the past. They were part of your team at some point in time and if they need help and if you can do something for them, you should always be willing to do so.

> ➤ **If your team member is rightful in asking/expecting something then do not hesitate to challenge old and existing policies and procedures.**

It is good to have well defined policies but while managing people, team leaders often come across situations which cannot be addressed by the existing policies. In such times, rather than just using the policy as an excuse not to do anything, it would be good to take things up with the Management based on the genuineness and get things done as an exception. Policies are meant to provide us with a framework, but they can never be expected to cover all possible situations that we might come across. Hence, if a request is genuine, then it must be treated as an exception and taken up based on its merits.

> ➤ **Do not commit to something that is not justified or is not possible.**

Committing to things to make team members happy momentarily or committing to something to get out of a sticky situation is a big trap and a very negative approach. Once a team leader/supervisor commits to something that is not possible, he not only loses the trust of his team member, but he loses the trust of the whole team and the organization.

While we talk about all the soft factors, it is very important for us to adopt the right approach to motivate employees and make them give their best in turn to the organization. Most often, a very blunt approach is adopted by some management/supervisors: "We pay them so they better work." Let us understand this in detail.

Space to Make Notes for Readers

_____

_____

_____

_____

_____

_____

_____

_____

_____

_____

_____

_____

_____

_____

Why Won't They Work
When We Pay Them?

When an employee joins, he expects more than just a salary from the organization. Infact, pay becomes incidental. People with potential and with intentions of staying for a longer period, expect much more. It is a fact that all employees spend more of their active/waking hours at work and not at home daily, except for weekends. For this reason, their expectations of much more than just pay stands justified.

All employees look forward to forming relationships (working relationships, good friends at work), a good work environment, earning more money, climbing up the corporate ladder, handling greater responsibilities and bigger teams, acquiring status in society due to their position at work, learning more and acquiring new skill sets.

When an employee joins an organization, the function and company becomes his second home. His desk becomes his personal space. This is why some organizations give employees an option to personalize their work area where they can display photos of their family members or decorate the space in a small way with calendars, personal pen holders, card organizers and decorative items. The other team members act as the employee's family in his second home. He establishes an equation with all of them and starts relating to them. While this may sound very basic, this process is very crucial for an employee to become a part of the team and organization.

It is not necessary to think beyond the statement, "We pay them so they better work," if the organization's objective is to extract work in the short run and then close the company or fire employees. But, if the organization intends to grow their business and have long-term business plans, it must discard this approach and think in terms of:

1. *Why will people join the organization?*

2. *What value can the organization add to people so that they stay for a longer period and give their best?*

3. *What can the organization do to become one of the best employers to work for and how to do it?*

4. *What value will the team member be able to add to themselves by working with the organization so that they become better professionals and human beings?*

5. *What is the organization going to give back to society/ community?*

This is an era of competition, competition in business, products, services and in hiring good employees too. Getting good, experienced, talented employees and retaining them is the most challenging task. Today, every organization wants to attract the best talent in the market by offering attractive salaries, perks, learning opportunities and growth plans. Gone are those days when an organization could attract people by just offering salaries.

An organization can get an employee to work by paying him a monthly salary, but it cannot expect the employee to give his best and think about the company's progress if he does not see any benefit in it for himself. One cannot expect employees to think beyond basics, stretch themselves when needed, take initiatives, be creative, or work towards increasing customer loyalty and profitability. The organization needs to have loyal employees who in turn will build loyal customers by going that extra mile. To put this in simple terms, it is not possible for an organization to have loyal customers if the organization does not have loyal employees.

Satish was working with my organization for a little more than 18 months and was given his first promotion. He was very skilled and an enthusiastic customer service personnel.

He wanted to improve on his quality scores all the time and would look out for opportunities to delight his customers.

One day, he got a call from a customer seeking assistance to make a deposit in his account. During their conversation, Satish realized that the customer was facing a problem with his computer keyboard. He was unable to type the amount to deposit on the web page. Any other associate in Satish's place would have advised the customer to get the hardware problem rectified and call the centre back. This would have been totally acceptable as per the standard operating procedure. Let us see what Satish did instead.

Satish guided the customer to use the computer mouse and type in the required amount on the calculator option in the accessories window, then asked the customer to copy the amount from the calculator window, paste it on the web page and helped the customer make the deposit.

The customer was very happy and sent a mail of appreciation on the level of commitment Satish had shown in resolving his problem with such a creative solution. What we have seen above is an example of out-of-the-box thinking, customer delight. This is possible when the employees are happy, motivated and passionate about their work and organization.

There has been a major shift in the work culture and management philosophy in the mid-90s. The ITES sector changed the job and employee engagement scenario totally and all other sectors around it started changing. The change was necessary for organizations to survive the competition as mentioned at the beginning of the chapter. No organization can aim to survive and remain profitable in the long run if it has employees leaving within a short period. Every time an employee leaves the organization, it costs money. (Cost in terms of hiring, administration cost, reputation in the market, training cost and re-hiring cost).

More importantly, it takes time to recruit, train the resource and for the resource to become productive. In addition to all this, it starts to drain the organization's knowledge base and resource pool. The longer period an employee works with the organization, it determines how cost effective the output will be. It also leads to reduction in the organization's running cost.

It is at this point that organizations started thinking and implementing measures to attract employees with higher salaries, better facilities, perks, training, and growth opportunities. All these measures intend to pamper employees, make them stay for a longer period and work up to their potential.

The objective is clearly two-fold:

1. **Get an employee to give his best**

2. **Make him work his best for a longer period with the organization.**

An organization needs to hire people for their positive attitude, experience, talent and passion. Once it has people on board, they need to be provided with complete training in their work area. When the organization has the right people, who have been completely trained, they need to be empowered within their scope of work. Empowerment makes employees accountable and responsible for the expected output. This induces a feeling of ownership in the employees. For their respective area of work, they become the owners and they strive to improve their output regularly so that they are among the best and are ahead of others.

***Whenever we empower our employees we need to necessarily have a strong monitoring and proper feedback mechanism so that we have indirect control on the output and we can initiate support or course correction.

Most people managing teams would have come across situations or team members, where one feels like telling them, "We pay you a salary so you better work." Every now and then, one will come across a few team members who come to work but they do not make any contribution. They spend their time chatting with others, gossiping, distracting other team members from their work or they browse the web and play games.

Every organization has its own way of correcting and dealing with such team members. Let me share with you one methodology:

Identify the reason: The team leader should talk to the team member. It would be best to have somebody with whom the team member shares a good equation, talk to the team member. It is important for the team leader to know and understand why the team member does not want to contribute. It is possible that the team member has some issues with his system, access to files/programs. He may not be confident of his ability to do the job. He may not feel comfortable in the team due to some issue with other team members or the supervisor. He may feel that his efforts are not recognized. He may have made up his mind to resign or he may have some personal problems due to which he is not able to concentrate on his work.

Once the team leader gets to know the reason, he needs to check if there is anything he can do from the organization's point of view to resolve the team member's problem. If anything can be done, then he needs to get it done as quickly as possible. Having one team member not contributing on a regular basis is a major dissatisfaction/de-motivating factor for other team members and it can be a bad influence.

If, after checking, the team leader concludes that there is no issue with the team member, he just does not want to work and is marking his attendance just for the salary, then he needs to initiate the performance improvement/course correction plan. The organization needs to inform the team member, what he can expect if he improves and what he should prepare himself for if his performance does not improve as per the discussion.

A general practice is not to give any team member more than two opportunities to improve their performance if they are far from the basic expectations. A team member with a skill gap is easier to manage and is an opportunity for training. On the other hand, a team member who is not motivated to work and does not want to learn and improve is a challenge, a challenge which needs to be dealt with quick action.

Bad performance or a decline in performance most of the times is due to de-motivation and there can be quite a few reasons. A few are mentioned below:

The team member feels that no matter how hard he works, he is not going to get anything more than his salary and this can happen due to three reasons:

1. **He feels that somebody who does not deserve it gets a good rating or promotion**

2. **He feels there is favouritism in the workplace, the boss is biased and his efforts will not earn him anything good.**

3. **Monotony or burn out.**

In the first two scenarios, it is important for the team leader/manager to be aware of the team member's issue. They need to speak to the team member and explain the scenario as soon as possible. If such cases are ignored or action is delayed, then they become a bad example and other team members get negatively influenced.

Sometimes a team member's performance declines due to monotony.

When Sunny asked one of his team members why his performance had dipped almost 20 % compared to his previous six months performance, the answer was, *"How long will I do this job of answering customer queries? I am sick of answering the same questions for the last two years"*.

In such cases one or a combination of the below mentioned suggestions can be used:

a. Advise the team member to change his career path if he does not like the current role.

b. Assign additional responsibilities along with his job but this will help only for some time.

c. Give him a small vacation.

d. Move the team member to some other function where he can use his skills.

e. Think of ways to make the daily work interesting. Maybe, you can assign other team members to be coached by this team member.

f. Start having contests based on best performers of the day/week/month and reward/recognition programs.

g. Move him to a function where he would be doing work that he finds interesting.

h. Let the team member know how he can move to higher positions in the same function by acquiring additional skill sets, if any.

i. Finally, if no other option works out, then the team leader needs to kick in the performance improvement/course correction process.

Be honest in addressing such issues with your team members even if it means telling them where they fall short. Do not avoid or postpone addressing such issues. By avoiding or postponing such issues, you not only waste your time and energy but also end up wasting the organization's time and money.

Remember one golden rule: "It is not what you say that hurts a team member but how you say it."

For Team Leaders/Supervisors

> **Never ever tell an employee that, "You get paid to work so you better do it."**

Try to create a sense of belonging and ownership and make them see what they gain by giving their best. It is the responsibility of the team leader to make the team members realize this and get them serious about their work or alternatively they should be shown the door.

A motivated employee contributes better than an employee who works only for the sake of salary. As team leader/manager, we need to constantly keep exploring ways and means to motivate our team members to get the best out of them, ensuring that the returns to team members in terms of rewards and growth is clear to all.

> **Set expectations for team members, notify them and document the same.**

We have discussed in the previous chapters the necessity and advantages of having a clearly laid down list of key deliverables. A formal and documented approach is better than discussion as far as Key Deliverables (KRA's or KPI) and these need to be discussed, explained and agreed upon by the team members before the start of the appraisal year for existing employees and for new employees as soon as they join.

> **A team leader needs to understand and must be sensitive about the team member's needs and career plans. Only then he would be able to get the best out of him.**

This we have discussed at length in the Employee Care segment. If you know what motivates the team members and what their aspirations are, then it becomes easy for you to motivate/guide and support team members to achieve those goals and in the process get the best out of them.

> **Set realistic targets for your team members.**

The targets should not be very easy to achieve and at the same time not impossible to achieve. The best way to get your team to accept and work on their targets is to make them a part of the goal setting/target setting exercise. When team members are part of the exercise, they will have clear understanding of how the target is arrived at and historical data of performance around the target so that they negotiate and accept the target. This is a healthier approach compared to imposing something on the team which creates doubt in their minds.

> **Induce a healthy competition among your team members. For some people competition is the biggest motivation.**

Competition, once triggered, is an ongoing motivation technique if it is kept healthy. In the absence of healthy competition at the workplace, the employee finds work very monotonous. Sometimes, a small push and nudge in the right direction makes employees outperform not only their peers but they surprise themselves about their own potential.

As a team leader/manager, identify the potential of your team members and grade them as per their potential and performance.

➢ **Let your team members know that they are an important and valuable part of the department. Discuss their contribution and its impact on the organizational goals.**

It is human to expect recognition and appreciation for one's work. If an employee knows how his contribution impacts the organizational goals, he feels that he is an important part of the organization and his role is pivotal. Everybody loves and wants to be a part of a success story and this pride can be a good motivation for employees to give their best.

➢ **Recognize and reward good performance with praise or monetary rewards, as per the performance.**

If the employee gets the deserved recognition and reward, it motivates him to do better. Rewards and recognition need not necessarily be in monetary terms always and can be done in the form of certificates, awards or a combination of both as per the performance level and impact of the team member's performance and in line with the policy/

philosophy of the organization. On the other hand, if an employee feels that no matter how well he performs it will not be noticed and recognized then he would not give his best and this can be a loss for the organization in terms of the opportunity/potential wasted.

➢ **Create your heroes**

Talk about them to your team members. At times, inspiration is a big motivating factor. All employees look out for instances and examples where the organization has recognized and rewarded outstanding performance. This acts as a source of inspiration for them. For an employee, the success story of their colleagues serves as an assurance that if they deliver outstanding performance, then their growth aspirations will be met in the organization. It also induces the feeling of competition/confidence in them: "If he could do it, then I can also do it".

➢ **A team leader needs to know the ticking points of his team members. Ticking points are the buttons of team members that when touched, motivates them.**

While we are on this subject, let us spend some time on understanding what ticks people?

Some people expect recognition for their excellent performance in the form of a fat bonus, while some do not find a fat bonus as motivating as praise in front of the whole company. A few get thrilled with the idea of getting a certificate for excellent performance which they can show to their family, friends and show in future interviews for a better job. Some people would not be happy with anything less than a promotion. A few others are thrilled with the idea of being recognized in the form of having a meal with their functional head or the CEO.

To sum it up, each team member craves for recognition in his own way. Some like it in purely material form, while others like it in the form of praise, a certificate, or additional responsibilities. Of course, there are a few who like recognition in all the ways mentioned above.

As a team leader, you have all the above options to use. You can pick up one or a combination of them, based on what is relevant to the situation/team member and his performance.

If a team leader understands what motivates his team members, then accordingly, rewards and recognition programs can be designed and announced which are in line with the organization policy. The scenario where an organization has an excellent Rewards and Recognition policy, but still most team members are below average performers or no team member qualifies for the R&R, indicates that the team leader/manager has not spent time to understand what ticks/motivates his team.

➢ **Give them due credit for the good work done.**

The team member needs to be assured that his performance is recorded and management is aware of his contribution.

A common problem is when team members feel that management is not aware of their contribution, as their only point of contact is the team leader/manager and they fear that credit will be stolen by the team leader/manager. A good practice in this regard would be to publish a weekly/monthly dashboard at the management level, which highlights the best performers of that period with their contribution details.

So now, the organization has adopted a very positive approach on how they treat their employees, they take care of them and try to do things to make the employees feel happy working in the organization. Now the challenge is, "How does the organization take care of the employees' growth aspirations?" Let us understand this in the following chapter.

Space to Make Notes for Readers

_____

_____

_____

_____

_____

_____

_____

_____

_____

_____

_____

_____

_____

_____

_____

_____

Should We Promote the Seniormost?

A good tenured resource is always an asset for an organization. At the same time, a bad tenured resource is a big liability and drain for any organization. We all know that not all tenured resources are necessarily the best performers. It is important for an organization to have quality resources and the qualities we should look out for are:

a. Skill

b. Talent

c. Right Attitude

d. Ability to adapt

e. Willingness to learn AND unlearn

+Tenure

All the above-mentioned qualities come into the picture, provided the required qualification criterion is met.

The weightage or priority of the above-mentioned qualities might vary from one job/role to another. Smartness is not bound by time frame or tenure. By saying this, one does not undermine the importance and significance of experience but not many of us would be comfortable with an employee's tenure being the sole criteria or being given very high weightage for any higher responsibility or growth.

Due to competition, most organizations have adopted the performance driven approach and experience has become just one of the factors. The focus is more on talent, capability, attitude, passion and experience. Tenure is an additional comforting factor. As organizations, we have slowly started shifting from the hard work approach to smart work. If this is the current approach of management, then this should reflect in the policy of the organization.

Imagine a scenario where an organization has an employee who wants to join the organization to give his best, he is very talented, capable and a very ambitious person. This employee joins the organization, performs his best and expects recognition and growth in return. *Don't you think it is fair on the employee's part to expect growth when he is capable, talented and has given his best?*

This employee in turn is informed by his higher ups that for his growth to the next level, he must necessarily serve in that position for a specific period. *What do you think the employee would do?* Now, to make things worse, the team member gets to know that some other team member, who is not on par with him in performance gets promoted, just because he has been with the organization for a longer period than him. The team member in all probability will resign and look out for a job elsewhere to fulfil his career aspirations. In this scenario, the manager is left with only two options:

1. **The manager allows the team member to resign. In this case, the organization loses out on an employee with talent, capability, and proven track record.**

2. **The manager makes an exception to promote the team member. Now, by doing this the team leader goes against the company's policy and in the process sends a conflicting message to the employees that the policies can be overlooked or changed anytime based on his discretion.**

The result of this would be that people who have been waiting for their turn as per tenure will oppose this decision and employees will lose trust in the organization and its policies.

We all know that getting a smart, talented employee is difficult and it becomes even more complicated when you expect the resource to be loyal and serve the organization for a long period by giving his best. If the organization has a promotion policy wherein higher weight age is given to tenure as mentioned in the scenario above, then why would good, smart, and talented people join or stay in the organization?

At the other end, there is another organization with a promotion policy purely based on performance. This organization will have two difficult scenarios to deal with on a regular basis:

1. If every year an employee is given growth based on outstanding performance, after a few years the organization will not be able to accommodate the growth aspirations of all employees and in turn will have a bunch of employees aspiring for the CEO chair.

2. The organization will have another problem where employees will join for a short period, leave after they climb up one or two levels based on performance and use the growth to negotiate a better pay/position in another company. The employees will start using the company as a launch pad for their career by performing above expectations for a short period, growing to the next level within the shortest possible time and negotiating with another organization for a higher level plus a good hike. If this happens, the organization will have a larger floating population compared to a stable and tenured resource pool.

Now that we have seen that following one of the two approaches has its own problems, what do we do as an organization?

It is possible for us to adopt an approach which is blended and has the benefits of both the above-mentioned approaches. As an organization, apart from the existing promotion policy, the organization can incorporate an additional **Fast Track Growth Policy.** The performance criteria should be at least 50 % above the normal target. If an employee delivers an exceptional performance which is 150 % of the normal performance on a consistent basis for two appraisal cycles, then he should be put on a Fast Track Growth Plan.

In this Fast Track Growth Plan, an employee would be nominated based on his exceptional performance and deputed for training and projects to enhance his skill sets for the next level. The employee will work closely with the next level personnel for a certain fixed period after the training, so that he gets hands on experience on the role he is expected to play post promotion.

The most important point would be the time frame an employee would take to get the promotion after delivering an exceptional performance. If the period is short, the employee would not be able to acquire the necessary skill sets and hands on experience and this would lead to his failure and in turn the team leader's/organization's failure. At the same time, if the period is long, the employee loses interest.

Recognition for good & exceptional performance, if delayed for a long period, loses its significance and the desired impact.

If the organization can have a single promotion policy as discussed above, it would be the ideal thing. The policy should assign more weightage to performance, capability for the next level, talent, skill set and lastly tenure.

Since tenure is a valuable aspect, it can be rewarded in terms of a good bonus. In order to meet employee aspirations, the organization can decide to give people a good variable pay/ bonus on their outstanding performance and link promotion to not just performance but to meeting skill set criteria required necessarily to move to the next level. They should provide the employee with an opportunity to add to their skill set by sponsoring the course or giving them lenience to complete the course. One key condition in the promotion policy should be availability of the role/position and in the absence of that, a suitable monetary reward can be given in the gap period.

An employee would leave his existing organization and join your organization for money, work culture and growth. *(Having a growth policy based on performance attracts the best talents in the market).* If the company does not provide growth or substantial recognition in form of monetary reward to smart, capable, and outstanding performers, why would a person with potential leave his existing organization and join another organization?

For Team Leaders/Supervisors

> ➤ **Recommend your best performers for growth but only if you are sure of their skill sets and capabilities.**

Sometimes, we end up promoting people solely based on performance. It is like one member of the cricket team has always been scoring centuries and we end up promoting that player as the team captain. Soon, we realize that this person has talent in batting but lacks other skills required to shoulder the responsibility of a captain, skills that include formulating game strategy, using his pool of players as per their core skills effectively, managing a team, leading in times of crisis, thinking for the team/match and series.

The solution to the above-mentioned scenario is that we move people to roles based on their performance but only if they have the required capability and skill sets for the next role/level. If the person does not have the required skill sets then we do not move him, till he acquires those skill sets or as an organization, we train the resource for the same.

We can help the team member by coaching or sending him for training and take a decision on completion of the same. If the company cannot support the team member for the training, then we need to provide the team member with feedback and encourage him to pursue such training on his own so that it will help him not only to grow but also to perform once he moves to that level.

I had one outstanding performer in my team and the team member's key strength was that he was a big number cruncher with a very good quality score. This team member had got an "outstanding performer" rating for two appraisal cycles in a row and we felt that this team member should be promoted. This team member was promoted, and it turned out to be a disaster for the team. The reason was simple: he had always known how to perform best as an individual. He did not have a clue about people management. He was rude and insensitive to his team members and would boss around. This resulted in unrest in the team and complaints started pouring in from all his team members.

Now, as a manager, I had only two options, either I ask this team member to change or leave. The other option was to train him, coach him on how to manage people. Coaching was a time-consuming option. Within that period of time other team members could get further de-motivated and leave the organization, so I had to go with the first option and I had to ask the team member to either change or leave.

➢ **Fight for your best performers, ensure that you have trained and tested them sufficiently before you move them to the next level.**

Let us look at another example.

A new member in my team, Kamal, had four years of experience in a hotel as a bartender and had all skill sets required for the role. He had made a shift from the hotel industry to the ITES sector, our company, due to better growth opportunities.

After about three months in the team, Kamal had proved to be a fast learner, a person willing to work long hours, learn and give his best to the organization. I sat in his feedback session and he had only one thing to say: "I switched from my previous industry with only one aspiration: career growth." All his supervisors gave positive feedback about his positive attitude, his willingness to learn, and willingness to accept challenges. I put him on a Fast Track Growth Plan, which was not a formal policy in the organization.

During the next 1 year, I assigned Kamal all possible challenging roles in the team, made him work in different shifts, made him conduct training for new batches, made him take all the internal process tests and gave him a new small batch for On the Job Training. While I was working on Kamal's career plan, he spoke to me one day about an internal job posting for a trainer in another department and he wanted my advice. I could understand his anxiety. He had been in the organization for more than a year (with prior experience of four years in his previous company) and he had not moved up by even a single level. If he applied for the internal job posting and got through, then he would move up one level immediately.

This is a testing moment for any manager, where he must give unbiased advice to his team member.

I told Kamal that if he applied for the internal job posting, he would get through and move up by one level, but he would end up moving away from doing what he was best at. His core skill was managing people, motivating people to outperform themselves and achieving targets. Instead, by accepting the job posting, his role would get limited to just training, which was an individual role and currently would be a dead end in the organization. I assured him that his performance was being monitored closely. He could expect more challenges and I would try my best to get for him what he deserved but I would not be able to promise him what level and the time frame. Kamal decided to go by my advice, trusted me and continued to give his best to the team.

By the time Kamal was due for his third appraisal, (the organization had a six month appraisal cycle) he was rated as an outstanding performer in the team; he had proved his capabilities in all spheres of work in the function. All team members felt that he truly deserved the promotion. I recommended him for a double promotion in that appraisal cycle. I had to fill up lot of data and provide enough evidence to top management and the HR team to justify the double promotion. The only word of caution that was given to me by management was that I should be able to handle the unrest if it crops up in the team. I was confident that nothing of that sort would happen and went ahead with the recommendation.

Finally, Kamal got the double promotion and was very happy. Neither any team member in my team, nor team members from other teams felt that the promotion was biased. Everyone in the team felt that the promotion was deserved. The biggest achievement for him apart from getting a double promotion was that it was the first time in the history of the company that somebody was given a double promotion.

In this case, it was a win-win situation for Kamal, the organization and for the manager. I identified potential, tested it, refined it, trained him, and gave him the deserved growth by making an exception.

- Test your team members by giving them projects or tasks related to the next level so that the team member not only gets a fair chance to prove himself but also will accept the outcome if he is not promoted. At the same time, you get an opportunity to re-confirm your decision.

- Do not recommend people for promotion just to please them or gain popularity but do so only based on competency and merit.

- Prepare your team members for the skill sets and capability, not necessarily for the next level but to enrich them and make them better professionals, so that when they go out in the market or to some other company, they don't fail and let down your company.

- Treat all your team members on par but give them only what their performance deserves.

Conduct the appraisal feedback session in a very formal, official manner so that the team member understands the seriousness of the process. For other routine feedbacks, one can use an informal methodology like, giving the feedback in the pantry while having lunch or over a cup of tea but the discussion needs to follow up with a summary recorded in a formal manner so that the discussion does not lose its significance and is considered as a general chat.

After going through all the previous chapters, it would be safe to say that now the organization is firing on all cylinders and exceeding their targets. But what if this is not happening? Why is it not happening and what does the organization do?

Let us try to understand this scenario in the following chapter.

Space to Make Notes for Readers

_____

_____

_____

_____

_____

_____

_____

_____

_____

_____

_____

_____

_____

_____

_____

Why Don't We Meet Our Goals When Everyone Is Working So Hard?

Having people to fill all the desks in the organization and be available for all the working hours is much easier when compared to ensuring all of them give the expected output consistently. How does the organization deal with a situation, where you have all the required employees and you have enough work for them, but they are not performing at the expected level or they are not working?

Are you familiar with a situation where an organization has a good tenured resource pool that works hard, but they still fall short of their targets? In this situation, one will find all employees coming to work and working all the time but still struggling to reach the target. Sometimes, in such situations, you will find that the employees appear to be busy too. Two possible reasons:

- The target is not realistic: One can review the past data or compare it with other teams and get the true picture. If required, do a detailed time and motion study to understand.

- Target is achievable and has been exceeded in the past. This should trigger the alarm for the manager.

*Target in this context denotes the expected output and need not necessarily be taken in the context of a sales organization.

In the first scenario, the solution is very simple; if the target is set too high and is not realistic, then the manager should discuss it, change it, and communicate the same back to the team. As discussed in the earlier chapters, the organization needs to set realistic targets. If the target is not within achievable limits, then employees will give up even before starting to work on it, as they have mentally not accepted the target.

Continuing with such unreasonable targets, will make the significance of a target disappear over time and the targets will not be taken seriously by the team. At the same time, if the target is very easy to achieve, employees do not find the target challenging or motivating and they find work boring.

In the second scenario, where the target is achievable, all the dynamics of people management come into play. The team leader needs to analyze and understand the reasons for the dip in team performance. There could be quite a few reasons which include:

1. There are a bunch of new team members and their contribution is not the same as tenured team members. New team members take time to exit the learning curve and deliver at the level of existing employees.

2. The target is not realistic in the current scenario. The change in scenario can be market driven, season driven or due to competition.

3. The team faces problems with the work tools or there is a problem with the reports or the reporting system.

4. The team is working but not performing up to their potential.

Of all the points mentioned above, the fourth point is an unhealthy sign for an organization. The rest of the points are self-explanatory. If we deep dive on this subject, we will be able to understand it much better.

The team is working but not performing up to their potential:

This situation means that all the team members come to work regularly as expected, but their contribution is not what it was in the past. In other words, their contribution falls short of the set target. Let us break this situation into small steps and understand it in detail:

- If a team has been achieving the same target earlier, then why would they be falling short now?

- What can lead to this situation?

- What does the organization do?

Why is the team falling short of the target now?

Before we get into details, we need to understand that this situation can come up in a new team chasing the target for the first time, based on the precedent set by some other team in the same organization or a team in a different organization. Alternatively, this situation can come up in an existing team with a proven track record of achieving this target in the past.

If this situation is to be dealt with in a newly set up team, we need to go back to the first three points mentioned above. Let us try to understand the situation of an existing team with a proven track record. In this kind of a situation, we find all team members come to work regularly. We also see them working at their desks for all the working hours, but we feel that the team is lacking the energy and the morale of the team is low.

What can lead to this situation?

This can happen due to several reasons:

- The team leader/supervisor has changed.

- The employee rewards and recognition policy has changed, or a change promised is long overdue.

- There is burn out in the team which has been overlooked.

- The team is de-motivated (this could be due to rewards, treatment, or recognition for the team or for individuals).

- The team members do not find any growth opportunities in the organization or they find very few opportunities to fulfil their career aspirations.

- It is also possible that suddenly there are better opportunities in the market and employees are waiting for their appraisal cycle to move out or barring a few team members, the rest of them are coming just for the sake of salary.

- Two bad things in this direction for an organization are: 1) False promises made by the Manager. 2) Employees losing trust in the organization and its policies due to any kind of favouritism or bias. In such cases, action should be taken on priority, although the result might take longer to achieve.

To reach the root cause of the problem, a team leader/ supervisor needs to have a discussion with all the team members individually, with the whole team together and identify the issues. Sometimes, the team leader needs to pick up indirect signals from team members, when they speak in a meeting, pantry discussions or during any general chat. The reasons and solutions will also vary based on the kind of business the organization is into. A sales-based organization has its own challenges when compared to another organization which is into collections or a call centre that provides customer support services.

What Does the Organization Do?

For any department or organization, dealing directly with revenue targets like sales or collections process, it is very important that the rewards and recognitions are done on a regular basis rather than doing it once a year. This is very important as the team member draws a lot of energy and motivation when he gets that regular pat/return in the form of a reward. The reward can be monetary or any other mode, but it is not ideal that in an environment where one must keep achieving targets month on month, the employee must wait till the year end for the reward.

The rewards and recognition can be broken down into small portions and disbursed monthly, while the major portion of it can be given during the year end. This serves as a monthly milestone for the team member and once he gets into the spirit of chasing, he would not need any pushing from the manager.

One Example:

I was a part of the collections team in an organization. All of us in the team used to have monthly targets. We were three executives, managing different collection agencies with different portfolios. Among the three of us, on a half yearly basis, the manager used to have an incentive scheme.

The executive who achieved the target and did the maximum collection for all six months (amount and percentage) or the cumulative figure over and above the target figure among the three, would get a prize (The prize was always a surprise). All of us would try our best to ensure that we get the prize, irrespective of what the prize would be. The reason was simple: It was a matter of pride that we had not only achieved but exceeded the target and this would also get us a better performance rating in the annual appraisal. The half yearly incentive scheme was conducted in the form of a team outing where one senior management member used to give away the prize.

Driving targets and monitoring them is relatively easier in the sales and collections field. It is a challenging task in the service sector due to the subjectivity and emotional quotient involved in it. In a sales and collections environment, figures determine the performance but in the service industry it is the customers' feelings, opinions or appreciation of the service that matter.

In the service sector, employees are not expected to achieve plain numbers, but they are expected to get high quality scores, high customer satisfaction scores or more compliments from internal and external customers. The performance yardstick gets more subjective. For instance, one employee would have dealt with the customer very politely and would have gone beyond his call of duty, but still the customer may not be delighted for various reasons. This is possible as we are trying to measure the feelings of a person and not a number.

A few things a Sales & Collections Organization can do in this regard:

➢ **Get to the root cause**

This can be done by holding meetings, discussions with the employees (meetings can be one-on-one or team meetings) or get an employee survey done by an external agency.

For Team Leaders/Supervisors

Spend time with your team members. This will give you some insight into the issues that are brewing in the team and a fair idea of their morale. This will also give you an opportunity to know the changes in the market scenario from the ground level. The way to do this is not by asking straight questions but by trying to strike light and general conversations with your team members and extracting the information.

➢ **Make an action plan and implement it without delay.**

Communicate back to your team about the management plans to implement the action plan and gather their feedback. This will, on one hand, help you reinforce confidence in the team members, regarding their issues being taken up seriously by management. On the other hand, you will get the opportunity to get feedback on the action plan. Communicate the action plan to your team in complete seriousness and let conviction reflect in your speech so that the team members get positive assurance from your communication.

> ➢ **Look at the attrition data of the last six months and check the reasons given by employees for leaving the organization.**

Most often the reason for low morale in team members is due to three reasons:

1. Unachievable target & unattractive incentive scheme

2. Issues with the direct supervisor or boss/team issue

3. Better opportunities in the market.

Once you can pinpoint the exact reason, dealing with it and coming up with an appropriate solution is easy. If you are not able to identify the exact issue, you will end up working in the wrong direction. Try to match the reason for leaving in the records with the information you have gathered at a personal level and only then you will be able to get to the exact reason.

> ➢ **Review the process of incentive schemes and the performance management system for fairness.**

If as a Team Leader, you want to have a stable and performing team, then you need to ensure that you conduct all evaluations for the team's incentive schemes and performance appraisal in a fair manner. In the absence of this, all your efforts in other directions will lead you nowhere.

As mentioned earlier, all your actions in this regard must reflect this motto: "To each as they truly deserve." This needs to be substantiated with data as and when required.

➢ **Gather information about the market and see if there is any significant change in the market.**

Communicate to your team members about the company's overall growth status and business plans. This will help the team members plan their career based on the company's performance and business plans. If the company is performing good, team members may not move out for fear of missing the opportunity to be a part of the growth. Market information will also help you reduce the gap in salaries of your team members, if not for all, at least for the best performers. Gather market information through both formal and informal channels so that you get the true picture.

➢ **Shuffle the portfolios/territories of the supervisors and if possible shuffle some employees also in the teams.**

A few changes in the portfolios and team will be refreshing for members and the team. If the changes are done keeping in mind the interest, skill set and capabilities of team members, it will show positive results. Such changes help in breaking the monotony.

> ➤ **Review the incentive program. If needed, make changes in it accordingly and communicate the same to the team diligently.**

The target and incentive scheme should be able to motivate team members and not scare them. The target should be challenging enough for a team member to feel good about achieving it. At the same time, the incentive should be rewarding enough to feel motivated and charged up. Let the team members know that the targets assigned are achievable. If possible, let them know the history, success stories, how it would benefit them in the short term and long term in the organization and in their career.

During my work tenure, I managed a collections team. We used to have targets for all the team members. The targets were divided into just two categories: one for new team members (less than six months in the organization) and one for seniors (above six months tenure). After a few months of implementation of the targets, we realized that most of the new employees had the potential to perform on par with the seniors within three months of joining but wouldn't do it as their targets set were only 30 % of the seniors.

We reviewed the targets and then implemented a slab system of three levels of target and added an incentive scheme. We divided the targets into three segments (Zero to three months, three to six months, six months and above). With the change in the target slabs and addition of the incentive scheme the results were outstanding.

➢   **If there is a burn out in the staff then organizing employee engagement events will help in breaking the monotony and re-energizing the employees.**

These events could be for a very small duration and can be conducted in the office during work hours by just taking employees off work for few minutes or it can be an evening outing with events followed by cocktail and dinner. These events must be in addition to the company-wide events which are held annually (These events can be scheduled on the weekends or public holidays so that work does not get disrupted).

This will help team members develop a bond with each other and will also provide them with an opportunity to iron out issues with each other in an informal manner and environment. Conduct small events involving all team members and help them mingle with each other.

➢   **Do not tolerate non-performance**

Conduct regular performance feedback meetings with your team members so that they understand how they are doing and where they stand in the organization's performance metrics. The objective of the meeting should be positive, to help team members understand how they are doing, where they need to improve and what support they can expect and finally, if the required improvement is not made, the course of action that would follow.

The below given points can be followed by a service-based organization in addition to the points mentioned above.

➢ **Run special programs like service week, quality week or employee of the week and declare the expectations and rewards.**

Design short term incentive schemes on a small scale like Customer Satisfaction Week/Month, Quality Performer of the Month, Star of the Month or the Maximum Achiever Award for the Month. Such initiatives create positive energy and enthusiasm in the team members. In the short term, these schemes will give good results. The rewards for such schemes can be as small as lunch with the manager, a gift voucher or a certificate displaying the name and achievement put up on the company notice board.

Small but meaningful things like these can be done by the manager and this is apart from the company-wide incentive scheme. Managers need to create a buzz about the special programs by putting up posters in the work area and notice board and talking about it in the meetings. This can also be done in a sales organization by declaring best performer of the month in terms of sales figures.

> ➢ **Look out for the main dissatisfaction factors from the Customer Satisfaction Survey Score or the Quality reports and make an action plan to deal with those factors.**

Try to analyze the Customer Satisfaction Survey Score/ Quality scores and understand the areas where majority of your team members are falling short of expectations and make an action plan to address those areas. Have regular team meetings and conduct relevant training programs. Present to them the plan versus achievements of the team along with the areas of concern. This will help the team members understand the gap in their performance and its impact on the team goals.

> ➢ **Conduct periodic review meetings.**

The focus of these meetings should be to review the plan versus actual performance, identify issues due to which the gap exists and arrive at a list of action points to fix those issues. As a team leader and manager, it is our job to help and support our team to meet their targets and step in to support whenever they get stuck and need support.

These meetings should be conducted weekly (assuming you have monthly targets) so that there is sufficient time available to do course correction, if required. Conducting such meetings regularly helps in setting the direction for the team. At the same time, it helps you make course correction jointly with your team members.

A presentation with graphs and metrics would be a good way of conducting this meeting.

These meetings need to necessarily have two-way communication so that the message is received and understood correctly. It also provides you with an opportunity to get to know the pressure points of your team members.

➢ **Pick up the best calls/service instances of your employees and play them to all the team members.**

Create a buzz among the team about the good service instances to pep them up. Success stories motivates team members, provides them with energy and direction. Let the team members know what is good about the instance and how it impacts the outcome and result. It would be good for the Team Leader/Manager to make team members understand the good things about the call/instance from all three perspectives: the customer, organization and the team member.

➢ **In the service industry there is a belief that a service personnel (be it in person or over phone) always needs to wear a smile and the customer can sense it in the tone of the person.**

The organization needs to constantly look out for reasons to boost the employee morale and give them reason to be cheerful and happy at work because

only when the employees are happy they will be able to put on a smile while they are on calls or serving customers in person.

Team Leaders need to do all the above-mentioned things to ensure that the team members enjoy their work and find enough reasons to be cheerful and motivated. There is no single point formula to make your team happy and cheerful. It starts right from the moment you walk into the office and depends on the atmosphere you create for your team members:

- Are they always tense, or do they always smile and enjoy their work?

- Are they terrified to make mistakes in the process of doing something different to satisfy the customer or do they know that if the mistake was made in the process of satisfying the customer, they will be supported instead of being reprimanded?

- Do they have a good friend at work? Do they look forward to coming to work every day?

- Are they totally policy bound and don't bother what the customer says or feels about the policies of the organization or how it affects him, or do they love to take initiatives and are very innovative in coming up with brilliant ideas to satisfy customers?

- Does your team member become stiff the moment he sees you or the Manager coming towards their desk or do they feel happy and wait to talk to the Manager about their last call?

If the team leader/manager can identify the reason for low employee morale, has done everything possible in that direction but still employees are not performing at the expected level, what does the organization do?

Space to Make Notes for Readers

_____

_____

_____

_____

_____

_____

_____

_____

_____

_____

_____

_____

_____

When to Let Go?

One of the biggest dilemmas in today's scenario for any organization is "to fire or not". On one hand, it is difficult to get resources and retain them, but on the other, attrition is a big drain on the company's knowledge and money. To top it all, the decision of firing, makes people management a complicated task.

Every organization has its own performance metrics, appraisal system and most of them lay down the process of termination. The difference is only in the stage at which the organization decides to kick in the process of termination, or in terms of the time an organization takes to make the final decision of terminating an employee.

Some organizations make this a part of the annual appraisal process, where employees scoring below a certain level are given time to demonstrate improvement in their performance, failing which they are terminated. During this process, they give enough time and support to the employee to improve his performance. At the end of the specified period, if the employee fails to improve then he is shown the door.

Few organizations do not wait till the appraisal process and do it based on the employee's monthly performance score and follow the same process as mentioned above.

Termination is immediate on grounds like lack of integrity, sexual harassment, embezzlement of funds, misusing company resources. Such terminations are simple, do not involve much thinking or subjectivity and are clearly defined in the form of a policy or code of conduct.

Terminations based on performance are more often debatable. At what stage does an organization take that call? There is an agreement in all organizations that one cannot keep unproductive resources for a long period of time, wasting the firm's money and resources.

A few common scenarios

- Employee fails to perform up to standards for more than a certain period.

- Employee fails to perform up to standards for more than one appraisal cycle.

- Employee performance has dipped and has been at a lower level for certain period.

- Employee has been given all the training required to perform the job but still is not able to perform. (This is more common in the case of new employees.)

- Employee commits errors leading to revenue/business loss to the organization.

- Employee does not report regularly to work for a certain period or takes frequent unplanned leaves.

- Employee provides customers with inaccurate information or incomplete solutions on a regular basis over a period.

- Employee fails to capture, or record information provided by the customer on a regular basis over a period.

- Employee has a habit of speaking rudely to customers.

As mentioned earlier, the debate is not if an organization needs to show its unproductive employees the door or not, but it is, at what stage does the organization do it and how they go about doing it in a fair and positive manner.

At what stage does an organization take the call to show the employee the door?

This depends on the kind of business or function the employee is working in. In a very critical function, it may not be possible for the employee to get more than one or even one chance to improve. In such cases, the training for the employee must be at that scale and adequate measures should be taken before the employee is put on the job. In all other functions, the organization needs to have a clearly laid down policy detailing the training period, time given to the employee before action will be taken, expected level of performance and details of the steps that will be taken in such instances.

Essential Points of the Policy

- Specify the training period.

- Lay down expectations of scores to be achieved in the tests conducted during the training.

- Detail the action that will follow in case of failure in such measures.

- Specify the On the Job Training period and expectations during that period.

- Every employee should be given their KRA's along with information on the minimum performance level expected.

- Specify action steps post first warning stage and review period.

- Final course of action.

The stage at which the final call of terminating an employee is taken is based on the nature of business of the organization, culture and values of the organization, the market situation, and the applicable laws. Most organizations prefer to give at least two chances to the employee performing below expectations before taking the final decision. These two chances can be over a period of two monthly feedback cycles or within the appraisal cycle.

Let us try to see if one can make the process of termination a positive one. If an employee has failed to perform in the initial stages then the manager needs to investigate:

- Recruitment process
- Training
- OJT process followed in the organization
- Check if all the employees from the new batch are not able to perform or only a few of them

This will help the organization to identify the areas where things are going wrong. Based on the findings, the organization can tighten the recruitment process, training, OJT process or get into a discussion with the employees failing to perform and understand the reasons. If only a few employees from the new batch are not able to perform up to expectations, then the issue is perhaps with their understanding levels, learning ability, interest in the job and commitment to the job.

If an employee has invested his time to go through the cycle of recruitment and training, then why is he not able to perform or why does he not want to perform up to the organization's expectations?

It is very important for the Manager to think along these lines and understand the frame of mind of the team member:

1. Gather feedback from training department which include regularity in training, interest and enthusiasm levels displayed by the team member, learning ability, test scores, attitude towards others and the organization.

2. Gather feedback as mentioned above from the coach responsible for the OJT.

3. Have a discussion with the team member regarding the feedback from the trainer and the coach and understand his view.

The discussions must be carried on with positive intention, to help the team member perform better and not just to find reasons to terminate him. Once the Manager has understood the issue with the team member, then he can accordingly draw an action plan with a reasonable time frame and appropriate support or additional training to help him get to speed.

Let Us Look at an Example

I had a new team member who joined the team with relevant experience and the required skill set. This team member had been an average learner during the training and OJT process. He was not able to complete his OJT process within the specified time frame, while all the other new team members from his batch had completed the OJT and started reporting to work.

All the seniors and team leaders gave up on this team member and concluded that he was a 'Wrong Hire.' The recruitment process had gone wrong in getting this team member on board and he needed to be terminated.

One Team Leader differed from the rest and approached me to assign this team member to his group and give him a time frame of one month as a last resort. After the completion of the time frame, to everybody's surprise, this new team member had made remarkable improvement and was performing on par with all the other associates.

What did this team leader do to turn around this employee?

During the agreed time frame of one month, the first thing that the Team Leader did was to strike an equation with the team member and understand him as a person. He realized that the team member was a little shy by nature and would hesitate to ask questions or clarify his doubts. This was a helpful clue for the team leader. He started working on the team member by sitting with him daily and taking him through the training topics for the first half of the day.

During the second half of the day, he used to provide him the practical experience by making him listen to calls relevant to the training topic and encouraging him to come up with questions in that regard. Gradually, the team member started opening up to the team leader and rather than just following instructions and the training manual, he understood the topics in totality.

As a result, after the stipulated period, he had developed a very good and in depth understanding of the process. This employee was one of the best performers among the top five in my team in the following appraisal cycle.

Another Example:

I was a sales executive during the early stages of my career. My sales numbers at the end of the month were only 40 % of the expected target. In terms of product knowledge, familiarity with the assigned territory and ability to communicate I was on par with all the other members of the team.

One day, my manager decided to come with me on sales calls and the first couple of calls he allowed me to talk while he took notes. My manager took me for a cup of tea and gave me feedback as per his observation and post tea, he took me again on sales calls, but this time he did the talking for the next three to four calls. From the next day onwards, I started displaying more confidence and in a couple of weeks I was performing on par with the other team members.

The above examples are good but not all cases turn out to be like this and the Manager must adopt the approach of **"Different strokes for Different folks."** It is very important for the Manager to get into the root cause of the employee's low performance. Terminating all employees not performing at the expected level would prove to be a costly short cut for the organization in the long run.

At the same time, the organization cannot waste time and resources on unproductive employees. The least that should be done in this regard is to get to understand the reason. Doing this may not necessarily help in that case but may help in making changes to the policy, process, and methodology and this will help in future.

Negative Indicators

- Employee has a very casual attitude despite being counselled and warned.

- Irregularity to work on a regular basis.

- Employee speaks rudely to customers and is not sensitive to customer needs.

- Lacks the required skill set or ability.

- Has an attitude problem.

Employees with the above-mentioned traits more often prove to be unproductive.

Things To Do

Check all the records of the team member in question:

- His attendance.

- His scores in the tests conducted during the training period.

- Feedback from the trainer about the enthusiasm level and interest level displayed by the team member.

- Feedback from the coach during the OJT period.

Speak to the team member and understand the problem from his side. Again, as mentioned earlier, no fault finding should be done. Instead, try to understand what could be done to help him perform better. Make a note of all the points and see if the team member needs additional time, training or coaching to get to the desired level.

It is more important for the organization to spend time and energy on employees who seriously intend to improve and who have the ability to learn. Do not waste time on employees who lack seriousness and are unable to learn or employees with a negative attitude. I personally believe in and follow this mantra: **"Skill gap can be tolerated and managed, but Will gap should not be tolerated."**

Provide the team member with the required support and set a time frame. Set review periods in between the time frame so that progress can be monitored. Let the team member also know the final action that will follow if he fails to improve. If the team member has skill set, abilities or interest not suitable for the role he has been appointed, then it would be helpful for the team leader and the organization to let the team member know that he would be better off in an organization where he could do what he is best at or what he is capable of doing better.

If the employee fails to improve and is asked to move out, then he needs to be given a fair feedback in the final discussion. This will help the team member understand his core skills, competency, and strengths apart from the weaknesses due to which he is being terminated. The team member can use this valuable information to decide & alter his career path if required.

For Team Leaders/Supervisors

The process of reducing the number of termination cases or to ensure that even the termination process is conducted positively, must start right from the training period of new employees.

> **Get involved with the new employees during the training stage.**

Efforts should be made to get to know them as a person and establish an equation with them. This will help the team leader get an understanding of the real person and not the image being portrayed to the outside world. Once he knows the real person, things will become much easier. We should put in our efforts to ensure that all new employees settle down and get comfortable in adjusting to the new organization. Once they are at ease and become a part of the organization, then they become more receptive to training.

➢ **Attend some of the training sessions with the new batch.**

This will help you get an understanding of the learning ability of the new team members, the seriousness being shown by them in regard to the job and will also give you some insight into the difficult topics in the process from the new employees' viewpoint. In addition to the above, you get to know the energy level and enthusiasm of each team member and this can make it very easy for you to assign different tasks/jobs within the team.

➢ **Ensure that the OJT process is smooth and it is more of hand holding rather than instructional.**

The OJT process is critical for a new employee. In this period, the new team member relates all the theoretical training to practical scenarios in the work area. At the same time, he is adjusting to the team and the environment.

If the employee finds any disconnect in the theoretical and practical scenarios or if he does not feel welcomed and comfortable in the team, then his concentration and performance is more likely to take a hit.

➢ **Monitor your team performance and keep giving timely feedback so that the employee can improve his performance.**

More often, team leaders wait for the feedback cycle to let their team members know that they are not performing up to expectations. This is like postmortem; you wait till the damage is done and then tell the team members about it. It would be a good practice to monitor the team performance on a regular basis, provide them with inputs the moment the performance dips so that they get time to improve before the formal feedback session.

The inputs need not be a full-fledged discussion but just a quick chat telling them where they stand and how much they fall short of expectation; it is just like giving a heads-up to the team member. During this time, you can also extend them support and arrange for help to improve their performance so that by the time you have a formal feedback session, the performance would likely have improved.

➢ **Communicate clearly and unequivocally in case of poor performance.**

During performance feedback, before you kick in the formal performance correction plan, communicate to the team member specifically:

- Where his performance falls short.
- Areas that he needs to work on.
- The permissible timeframe.
- The action that will follow in case of failure to improve.

This is better than beating around the bush to arrive at the imminent assessment. Clear communication in such instances will help the team member understand the seriousness of the situation and provide him with clear direction.

➤   **Explore unconventional possibilities.**

Finally, based on the team leader's observation and feedback collected from various sources including the immediate supervisor, the quality team, the trainer and HR about the team member in question, explore the possibility of maybe assigning a new coach, changing the team member's shift or team from the fold of one supervisor to another or anything else that may help the team member to do better. Give him a short vacation if you sense a burnout.

> At times, such small steps help a team member to get back his focus on the job and improve his performance. It is always better to check all options and exhaust them before you take the final call to terminate the employee. It can save the cost and effort of recruiting new employees. It would be good if it can be avoided altogether or at least reduced to some extent.

> This does not mean that the team leader should end up wasting the organization's time and money trying to convert one unproductive resource to a productive

resource, but if all these steps are incorporated in the policy then the amount of time wasted will reduce.

Even while having the final discussion, ensure that the employee is treated with all due respect and is not looked down upon by any department during his exit.

I thank all my team members for providing me with such a good learning experience that I could think of writing this book.

Space to Make Notes for Readers

About the Author

Shashikant Dabral, by birth a Garhwali but a pure Hyderabadi at heart, is a postgraduate in Industrial Relations and Personnel Management. He has 25 years of work experience in various streams including Sales, Customer  Service, Training, Credit and Fraud Control, and managing diverse background teams in a BPO environment. He has 21 years of rich experience in building and managing teams. During his career, he has managed teams of different nationalities, from different dialects and size ranging from a team of 80 to 1200 team members, spread over multiple locations in India. He has managed multiple processes in a captive international BPO. He also served as the Centre Head for a domestic call centre in India.

During his work tenure, he had the opportunity to work with a couple of multinational organizations right from their launch to a fully grown, profit-making company. It was in these organizations that he had the opportunity to understand and test his skills on people management, as these organizations provided him with valuable learnings on recruitment, launching a new process, building a cohesive team, dealing with people issues and managing a team. He can be contacted at shashikantdabral@gmail.com.

www.ingramcontent.com/pod-product-compliance
Lightning Source LLC
Chambersburg PA
CBHW030626220526
45463CB00004B/1429